MULBERRY

Reaktion's Botanical series is the first of its kind, integrating horticultural and botanical writing with a broader account of the cultural and social impact of trees, plants and flowers.

Published
Apple Marcia Reiss
Bamboo Susanne Lucas
Birch Anna Lewington
Cactus Dan Torre
Cannabis Chris Duvall
Carnation Twigs Way
Carnivorous Plants Dan Torre
Geranium Kasia Boddy
Grasses Stephen A. Harris
Lily Marcia Reiss
Mulberry Peter Coles
Oak Peter Young
Palm Fred Gray
Pine Laura Mason
Poppy Andrew Lack
Primrose Elizabeth Lawson
Rhododendron Richard Milne
Rose Catherine Horwood
Snowdrop Gail Harland
Sunflowers Stephen A. Harris
Tulip Celia Fisher
Weeds Nina Edwards
Willow Alison Syme
Yew Fred Hageneder

MULBERRY

Peter Coles

REAKTION BOOKS

In memory of my lifelong friend, Geoff Appleton

Published by
REAKTION BOOKS LTD
Unit 32, Waterside
44–48 Wharf Road
London N1 7UX, UK

www.reaktionbooks.co.uk

First published 2019

Copyright © Peter Coles 2019

All rights reserved
No part of this publication may be reproduced, stored in a retrieval system, or transmitted, in any form or by any means, electronic, mechanical, photocopying, recording or otherwise, without the prior permission of the publishers

Printed and bound in China

A catalogue record for this book is available from the British Library

ISBN 978 1 78914 142 9

Contents

Introduction 7
one Black, White and Red 19
two Mulberries and Silk 53
three Lost Angels 85
four Mulberry Mania 112
five Art, Legend and Literature 147
six Tree of Plenty 179

Timeline 222
References 233
Further Reading 246
Associations and Websites 247
Acknowledgements 248
Photo Acknowledgements 249
Index 251

Ancient black mulberry in Italy, 2010.

Introduction

Like most cousins, the three main species of mulberry tree – black, white and red – have very different personalities, even though they are from the same family. The red mulberry (*Morus rubra*), which is native to North America, tends to be tall, doesn't travel much and, as it happens, is not faring very well. The black and the white mulberry, in contrast, are globetrotters. Neither grows much taller than 10 metres (33 ft), and both are thriving. Their characters, however, couldn't be more different.

If the black mulberry (*Morus nigra*) were human, it might be described as stubborn, self-contained, a loner – but also wise, generous and full of character. Despite countless millennia on the planet, the black mulberry has produced almost no significant variations, except in the size and shape of its fruit. It categorically refuses to mix with other mulberry species yet, paradoxically, has more sets of chromosomes in each of its cells than any other flowering plant. It has travelled from its original home in Persia (modern Iran), Central Asia and the eastern Mediterranean, to North America and every country in Europe – but has never really settled in Asia.

The white mulberry (*Morus alba*) is almost the opposite. In human terms, it would be sociable, a good mixer, adaptable, self-effacing, loyal and used to being of service to others.

Native to East Asia and the lowland forests of the Himalayas, it is now found on every continent of the globe and has so many varieties and subspecies that no one knows exactly how many there are.

The white mulberry will interbreed easily, to such an extent that it is threatening the long-term future of America's native red mulberry as a separate species.

In its native China, the white mulberry is the stuff of legend. It is an *axis mundi*, the birthplace of the ten suns. No other tree has played a greater role in the economic and cultural prosperity of so many civilizations, for so many centuries. The leaves of the white mulberry are the only source of food for the larvae of a blind, flightless, domesticated moth, *Bombyx mori*. But *Bombyx mori* is no ordinary moth and its larvae no ordinary caterpillars. When they are ready to pupate, the larvae spin cocoons of raw silk, earning them the soubriquet 'silkworms'. Even today, despite the development of synthetic fibres like rayon in the late nineteenth century, global trade in cocoons of raw silk is worth over U.S.$1.7 billion a year.[1]

The Chinese, who discovered how to make silk 4,700 years ago, held a monopoly on the process for over 2,500 years – along with

Illustration by E. Srellett, 1909. The bush in the nursery rhyme 'Here we go round the mulberry bush' was probably originally a blackberry or bramble bush, not mulberry.

Introduction

Maria Sibylla Merian, 'Mulberry leaf, silkworm, cocoon', in *De Europische Insecten* (1730).

the vital role of the modest mulberry tree. Silk manufacture in China was one of the main drivers of traffic along the network of routes that became known as the Silk Road, albeit a misnomer. This network, which pre-dated the discovery of silk by centuries, also conveyed jade, jewels, gold, camels, ideas, religions, technologies – and people.[2] It was also, without doubt, the original conduit for the introduction of *Morus alba* westwards beyond its natural range.[3]

While silkworms will feed on the leaves of the black mulberry, the resulting silk is coarser and the caterpillars do not prosper so well as on a diet of white mulberry leaves. As the integrated agricultural techniques for producing silk thread (known as 'sericulture')[4] spread outside of China from the second century BCE, the white mulberry eventually caught up with them, if it was not there already.

The link between mulberry and silk has often eclipsed the tree itself, reducing it to an organic leaf factory, whose only function is to fuel the silk industry. The most common Chinese white mulberry species was even known at one time as the 'silky mulberry' (*Morus bombycis*). The idea of a leaf factory is not an exaggeration – cloned mulberries can be grown in vast plantations of up to 25,000 trees, pruned to shoulder height and mechanically harvested of their leaves. These manicured shrubs are a far cry from the magnificent trees that old mulberries can become, like the *kalprivsh* or Holy Tree, in the Joshimath Valley in the Indian Himalayas, with a trunk 21.5 metres (70.5 ft) in girth, and reputed to be over 1,200 years old.[5]

For a few hundred years, until the white mulberry caught up with the introduction of sericulture to the eastern Mediterranean, the leaves of the native black mulberry were used to feed silkworms. The famous silks of the middle to late Byzantine Empire (sixth to early fifteenth centuries), as well as those of Persia, Greece, Spain, Sicily, Italy and France, all got started with silkworms fed on the leaves of the black mulberry. The Moors introduced *Morus nigra* to southern Spain and North Africa in the tenth century, along with sericulture. Even James I's (failed) attempt to start a silk industry in England in the early seventeenth century was reliant on black mulberry trees imported from France.

The black mulberry, though, is not a 'natural' when it comes to industrialized agriculture. It is more of a solitary tree, at least after millennia of domestication. The signature of *M. nigra*, along with its celebrated shade, is its blood-red, juicy fruit, which has stimulated the imagination of poets since antiquity. With a tart sweetness not unlike red wine, the fruit turns to mush almost as soon as it is picked. It cannot be dried or transported and only makes its way to market when trees are close by. The Romans knew this and planted black mulberries in southern England, France and Germany when they settled there about 2,000 years ago. Rich in antioxidants and other active ingredients, the black mulberry was commonly planted in the infirmary gardens of medieval monasteries. Entire orchards weren't necessary – a single mature tree can produce more fruit than even a full monastery of sick monks could consume.

Introduction

Morus nigra has heavy spreading branches and often leans at an angle. Hampstead cemetery, London, 2017.

The fruit of the white mulberry, by contrast, is pale by name, bland by nature. It has been described as 'insipid' but has the commercial virtue of being easy to dry, store, transport and commercialize. It is an ingredient of traditional Chinese medicine and is commonly used as a sweetener in cooking. Dried white mulberry fruit is sent from Southeast Asia and Turkey all over the world. The species just can't help going global.

For all its modesty though, *Morus alba* has acquired a reputation for producing the most expensive wood in the world. A few rare trees on just two volcanic islands in the Pacific Ocean, south of Tokyo, yield a golden timber with a dense grain and a unique capacity to

Veteran *Morus alba*, Longwood Gardens, Kennett Square, Pennsylvania, 2009.

shine, known as 'chatoyance'. This has made it the wood of choice for Japanese master cabinetmakers and it was once reserved solely for the Imperial family.[6]

Sericulture transformed landscapes not just across much of China and Japan, but also from Persia to Piedmont and from Provence to Pennsylvania. A whole region of Greece even got its name (Morea – now the Peloponnese peninsula) from the mulberry, possibly because it is shaped like a mulberry (*Morus*) leaf or because of the quantity of (black) mulberries that once grew there.

Introduction

The fortunes of silk industries have risen and fallen over the millennia as empires and nations waxed and waned. At one time, high-quality silk was more likely to come out of Italy than China. Yet the global cycle of sericulture has now returned to its original home in China and India (where non-mulberry silk also goes back 4,500 years). The collapse of European and American silk industries in the nineteenth century (following a decimating silkworm disease) has left behind terraces of neglected mulberry trees, while centenarian trees today stand in the courtyards of old farmhouses (sometimes converted to boutique hotels), or as pollards lining rural roads and village streets. In some cases all that remains is the name – Mulberry Street in New York City's Lower Manhattan, Mulberry Walk in London's Chelsea, the Place du Mûrier in the Saint-Maur suburb of Paris, all evoke memories of long-lost mulberry plantations.

Across London and some other cities in England, the descendants of mulberry trees planted during James I's abortive attempt at sericulture four hundred years ago are now living testimony to a long-disappeared past, often growing in the most surprising places, surrounded by layers of urban development. These old trees have come to be strongly associated with a sense of place and identity for local communities. They can be landmarks, places for children to play – and, in summer, to clamber among the branches and shake down the ripe fruit. And they can keep alive urban myths, such as a belief that it was in an old mulberry tree on Peckham Rye in south London that the English poet William Blake witnessed a vision of stars and angels. There is Milton's mulberry in Cambridge, Keats's mulberry in northwest London, Peter the Great's mulberry in Deptford and Bishop Bonner's mulberry in Bethnal Green (London's former silk-worker district).

The task of dating these 'historic' black mulberries can be something of a trap. The tendency of *M. nigra* to grow rapidly, develop a thick trunk with lumps, bumps and burrs, to lean or topple over, gives

Overleaf: This collapsed black mulberry tree may be as old as the Tudor house it belongs to in Suffolk (England).

these trees an ancient appearance, even when they are still relatively young. The late British dendrologist Alan Mitchell famously dated an ancient-looking black mulberry at East Bergholt Place in Suffolk as being three hundred years old, based on the circumference of its trunk. As it turned out, it had been planted just 64 years earlier, on the day its present owner was born.[7]

Some white mulberries, which are often said not to live as long as black mulberries, can reach an astonishing age. The remote Ogasawara (or Bonin) Islands, 1,000 kilometres (620 mi.) south of Tokyo, are home to a unique, endemic species of white mulberry, *Morus boninensis*, unknown (at least in the West) until the nineteenth century. A ring-count of a stump discovered on one of the islands established that it was over 2,800 years old. Sadly, after a century of logging and hybridization with the introduced white mulberry, the species has almost become extinct.

The paper mulberry, which we also discuss in this book, is really more of an honorary family member. No longer considered a *Morus* species, its taxonomic name has shifted from *Morus papyrifera* to

Morus boninensis is endemic to the Bonin (Ogasawara) Islands of Japan. A stump on one island had a ring count of 2,800.

Introduction

Broussonetia papyrifera. It is valued for its bark and has been used for centuries in China, Japan, Korea and the Pacific Islands to produce textiles and paper – including the first paper money, often mixed with bark from *Morus alba*.[8]

The first chapter of this book looks in greater depth at some of the defining characteristics of the main species of mulberry – black, white and red, as well as the paper mulberry. A book on trees has to have a bit of botany. Chapter Two pays homage to the extraordinary arranged marriage between the mulberry and the silkworm to produce silk on an industrial scale, tracing its origins back to Neolithic China and the beginnings of its slow march westwards. Chapter Three looks at the black mulberry in its native lands, as well as the way that it, too, was harnessed for a while to service nascent silk industries. Chapter Four shows how the migration of the mulberry for sericulture was often accompanied by exiled silk weavers fleeing religious or ethnic persecution. Chapter Five moves away from silk to look at the ways in which the mulberry has inspired artists and writers since antiquity. And, finally, Chapter Six highlights some of the enormous range of uses to which the mulberry has been, and continues to be put: from a humble mouthwash to the most exquisite wooden objects used in the Japanese tea ceremony.

In writing this book there has been a continual temptation to hitch the mulberry once again to silk and to get lost in the latter's exotic, seductive history. I have tried to resist this temptation and to bring the focus back to these revered trees for their own sake; to honour their inherent beauty – individually and collectively – and their claims to a place alongside other champions in the universe of trees. In other words, to tell the story (or stories) of the mulberry.

The berries of the black mulberry are 'syncarps' or clusters of tiny fruits (drupes). The flowers are catkins and can be male or female, often on the same tree. Drawing by B. Thanner, in Johannes Zorn, *Icones plantarum medicinalium* (1780).

one
Black, White and Red

The mulberry genus, *Morus*, first emerged about 63.5 million years ago and belongs to the large *Moraceae* family of tropical and temperate flowering plants, which is divided into 37 genera and an estimated 1,179 species, including the common fig (*Ficus carica*), whose leaves have a similar shape to the lobed leaves of white mulberries and those on some young black mulberry shoots.

There is some confusion over the exact number of distinct species of mulberry, as different names are often used for the same species. According to the Kew Plant List,[1] of the 217 plant names recorded under the mulberry genus (*Morus*), just seventeen are accepted as genuinely distinct species. The others are either different names for the same species, or still in need of further clarification. A recent genomic analysis has even suggested that there may only be eight truly distinct species: *M. alba*, *M. nigra*, *M. notabilis*, *M. celtidifolia*, *M. serrata*, *M. insignis*, *M. rubra* and *M. mesoygia*.[2]

In 1607, an English scholar, Nicholas Geffe, translated what was then the definitive treatise on the cultivation of mulberry trees to feed silkworms and the making of silk thread from their cocoons, first published in French in 1599 by the French agronomist and royal silkworm expert, Olivier de Serres (who also improved the greenhouse, coincidentally known in French as a *serre*).[3] In Geffe's translation, entitled *The Perfect Use of Silk-wormes, and their Benefit*, Serres succinctly describes the two main 'races' of the *Morus* genus that were known at the time.[4] It would be difficult to pack more information about the mulberry into a hundred words than Serres does:

> There are two races of Mulberries discerned by these words, blacke and white, discordant in wood, leafe and fruite: having nevertheless that in common to spring late, the dangers of coldes being past, and of their leaves to nourish the Silk-worme. One sees but one sort of the blacke Mulberries the woode whereof is solid and strong, the leaf large and rude in the handling, the fruit blacke, great, and good to eate. But of the white, there is manifestly knowne three *species*, or sortes, distinguished by the onely colour of the fruit, which is white, blacke, and red.[5]

While it is true that some species of white mulberry produce white fruit, and black mulberries produce a very dark purple fruit, the colour of the fruit is not a reliable key to its identification. Some species of white mulberry produce black fruit, while the fruit of the red mulberry turns dark purple. The distinction of 'black' (*nigra*) and 'white' (*alba*) species is in fact based on the colour of the buds – light brown for the white and dark brown/black for the black mulberry. However, as black and white were the only two species known outside of Asia when English settlers first arrived in Virginia in 1607 and found a new species, they named it the red mulberry (*Morus rubra*), this time on the basis of the dark red colour of its fruit.

By far the majority of mulberry taxa are naturally occurring varieties or cultivars (cultivated varieties) of the white mulberry, though. Several of the commonly recognized white mulberry species, like the Japanese mulberry (*Morus japonica*), Indian mulberry (*Morus indica*), wild Korean mulberry (*Morus australis*) and Chinese mulberry (*Morus multicaulis*) are closely related. To this list, William Bean, in his classic compendium *Trees and Shrubs* (now an online database), adds *Morus cathayana*, which is native to central China.[6] They are all widely used for silk manufacture. The so-called paper mulberry (*Morus papyrifera*,

M. nigra does not usually grow much over 10–12 metres.

or *Broussonetia papyrifera*) is valued for its bark, which has long been used in China, Japan, Korea and some Pacific islands to produce paper, but is no longer considered a member of the *Morus* genus.

The Chinese have had names for many naturally occurring varieties of white mulberry for centuries, but there is little mention of the black mulberry in Chinese writing. The opposite is the case in Europe, where the white mulberry only arrived in the fifteenth century and early records only refer to the black mulberry.

Francisco José Domingo, 'Morus alba latifolia', in Francisco Manuel Blanco, *Flora de Filipinas* (1880–83).

The Wisest of Trees

In his *Natural History* the first-century CE Roman naturalist Pliny the Elder noted the tendency of the mulberry to 'spring late':

> [the mulberry] buds the latest among cultivated trees and only when the cold weather is over, owing to which it has been called the wisest of trees [*sapientissima arborum*]; but when its budding has begun it breaks out all over the tree so completely that it is completed in a single night with a veritable crackling.[7]

Pliny's claim that mulberry leaves burst forth noisily in one night needs to be taken with a pinch of salt. It is true that leaf flushing is closely synchronized and can occur almost simultaneously throughout a given tree – and even across neighbouring trees. Whether or not it can be heard is a moot point.

Pliny's 'wisest of trees' epithet for the mulberry was well observed, however, and has passed into modern gardening lore. The English Edwardian gardener 'Gussie' Bowles, best known for developing new crocus cultivars, regularly used the late-spring leaf flushing of the black mulberry in his garden at Myddelton House, north London, as reassurance that 'those plaguey Ice Saints have finished playing fool with the weather.'[8]

The very name of the mulberry genus, *Morus*, came to be associated with this late flushing. This originally came from the Proto-Indo-European root, *moro*, meaning a black berry. This became *móron* in ancient Greek, and *morum* in Latin, both meaning the black mulberry. A fondness for playing with homonyms led the ancients to associate the mulberry with delay (the Latin *mora*) and being slow (the Greek *moros*). Ironically for the wisest of trees, *mora* also came to mean 'foolish'. The mulberry, then, is wise for being slow in putting out its leaves. Much has been made of this oxymoron, the wise–foolish mulberry. Interestingly, the very word 'oxymoron' means sharp–dull,

Black mulberry buds (closed).

Black mulberry bud (opening).

Black mulberry leaf (emerging).

Black mulberry leaf (open).
Pliny the Elder claimed that mulberry buds open suddenly with a cracking noise – but only when the last frost has passed.

Morus alba pendula (weeping white mulberry), St Nicholas Church, Deptford, London.

or wise–foolish, from the Greek *oksús* (sharp) and *mōros* (slow or foolish).[9] The *morus* root has persisted in the translation of mulberry in many languages: *mûre/mûrier* (French), *Mauerbaum* (German), *Moerbelieboom* (Low Dutch), *merenn* (Middle Irish), *merwydden* (Welsh) – and the Old English term 'murrey' was used as the name for the dark purple colour of the black mulberry fruit.

Another common feature of black and white mulberries, as Serres was already aware, is that the leaves of both species can be used to 'nourish the Silk-worme'. Until the white mulberry was introduced from China into countries around the Caspian, Black and Mediterranean Seas, from Persia and Turkey to Greece and Italy, they used the leaves of their native black mulberry to develop lucrative silk industries. As the Estonian social historian Victor Hehn remarks in his fascinating and quirky book, *Cultivated Plants and Domesticated Animals in their Migration from Asia to Europe*, published in 1885:

[The black mulberry's] first planters, who thought nothing but of the dark berries, little dreamt that one day the rough leaves would, by a manifold metamorphosis through a small caterpillar, be changed into a soft, glistening costly tissue.[10]

Thus when James I of England tried to start a silk industry in 1609 using the black mulberry, his choice was not misguided, as has often been claimed. But, when the white mulberry did eventually begin to be used in Europe for sericulture, its leaves gradually ousted those of the black mulberry everywhere as the staple food for hungry, commercial silkworms.

The Black Mulberry

The black mulberry is a deciduous tree, most easily identified by its reddish, heavily ridged bark, which is often gnarled with large burrs. It has a tendency to lean at a pronounced angle, like the Tower of Pisa. Mature trees are often almost as wide across the crown as they are high (7–12 metres, or 23–40 ft), making them celebrated for their shade. Black mulberries grow quite quickly at first, especially if they are propagated using the traditional 'truncheon' technique (from the French *tronçon*), where a length of branch the size of a man's arm from a mature tree is pushed deep into the ground. Young shoots will sprout from the sawn-off top of the truncheon, often giving the tree a characteristic 'Y' shape, with two trunks later growing up from the older bole. Trees propagated from truncheons grow more quickly and will fruit earlier than those propagated from seed or 'slips' (cuttings). These slips are grafted onto older root-stock, which, interestingly, doesn't have to be the same species.

The gnarled trunk and thick, spreading branches give even fifty-year-old trees the appearance of being much older. Leaning mature trees often eventually collapse under the weight of these long, heavy branches, unless they are supported on props. Branches that touch the ground but do not break off will often put down roots. Several of the veteran specimens found in old English gardens and parks are now completely horizontal, with branches forming multiple new trunks.

The sixteenth-century English botanist John Gerard, in his *Herball; or, Historie of Plantes* (1597), described the black mulberry with enviable conciseness:

> The common Mulberrie tree is high and full of boughs: the bodie thereof is many times great; the barke rugged; and that of the roote yellow; the leaves are broade and sharpe pointed; something harde, and nicked on the edges; in steed of flowers, are blowings or catkins, which are downie; the fruite is long, made up of a number of little grains, like unto a blacke Berrie, but thicker, yet is the iuice whereof it is full, red: the roote is parted many waies.[11]

His contemporary, the doctor, apothecary and botanist William Turner, was equally pithy:

> The mulberry tre hath leves allmoste roude saving ye they are a lytle sharp at ye ende. They are indented about ye edges after the maner of mynte. It hath hoary Floures & a fruite in proportion som thing long. In color when it cometh first furth whyte in cotinuare of tyme it waxeth rede and after warde when it is full rype it is blacke.[12]

Fruit

The fruit of the mulberry resembles an elongated blackberry, but is really a 'syncarp' or aggregate of about twenty small fruits called 'drupes', or 'drupelets'. Each drupelet is a fruit, with flesh surrounding a pip with a seed inside, and develops from one of the clustered ovaries that make up the female catkin. Miles Hadfield, a writer on gardens and founder of the UK Garden History Society, graphically described the female catkin as 'a cluster of green barnacles with white, silky tentacles: these swell up and become the juicy fruit we eat'.[13] The female catkin resembles the final fruit cluster in shape and can be identified by these 'tentacles' – in fact a pair of thin white pistils standing up like bunny ears, or the feelers of an insect, on each individual drupelet. These collect pollen from male catkins, which are 1–2 centimetres (0.4–0.8 in.) long and hang down from the leaf axil. They appear hairy, because of the pollen-bearing stamens.

Some black mulberries are hermaphrodite – they have both male and female flowers on the same tree (that is, they are 'monoecious') – and can pollinate themselves, while others have male and female flowers on separate trees (they are 'dioecious'). Trees bearing female catkins alone will only produce fruit with fertile seeds if there is a male tree nearby. However, they can still go on to produce infertile and seedless fruit, even without being pollinated. Because of the purple stains caused by falling fruit, black mulberries are not often planted as street trees, unlike the white mulberry. When they do plant them, urban planners tend to use male trees, which do not develop fruit.

Mulberry slips grafted onto rootstock.

181. Morus nigra L. Schwarzer Maulbeerbaum.

The fruit of *Morus nigra* start off green, turning red then dark purple as they ripen. The inset (5) at top left shows the female flower, with its forked stigma, short style and spherical ovary. Male flowers (1 and 2) have four anthers which bear the pollen.

Because the clustered fruit of the black mulberry bears a superficial resemblance to the blackberry (or bramble), the same name was used for both kinds of fruit in classical times (*mora* or *moron* in Greek and Latin). To avoid confusion, the mulberry fruit would be referred to as *morum celsae arboris* (the mulberry of the tall tree), and the tree itself as *morus celsa*. The modern Italian word for mulberry, *gelso*, probably derives from this root.[14] In its native lands (or at least where it was introduced a very long time ago), *Morus nigra* is renowned for these juicy, purple-black fruit, which have a delicious, mellow tartness that resembles red wine. In Central and South Asia and the Middle East, these trees and their prized fruit are still known by their old Persian name *shahtoot* (*toot* means 'mulberry' and *shah*, 'kingly', 'superior'), or derivatives, such as *shajarat tukki* in Arabic. The introduced white mulberry, now also common in modern-day Persia (Iran), is known simply as *toot*.

Within a short time after they are picked, black mulberries notoriously turn to a blood-red mush: 'Now humble as the ripest mulberry/ That will not hold the handling', says Volumina, in Shakespeare's *Coriolanus*. To minimize this, in the hot Mediterranean summer the Roman lyric poet Horace (Quintus Horatius Flaccus), writing in the early part of the first century CE, recommended picking mulberries in the morning:

> I'll give him Health, who when his Meals are done,
> Eats juicy Mulberries, pluck'd before the Sun
> Doth rise too high, and scorch with heat of Noon.[15]

Visitors to the queen's summer garden parties at Buckingham Palace are literally caught red-handed when they have surreptitiously picked black mulberries from the National Mulberry Collection, now housed there in memory of the Mulberry Garden planted by James I in the early seventeenth century, but grubbed out two hundred years ago.

Unlike the fruit of the white mulberry, black mulberries cannot be dried and stored. They are rarely found in markets or shops even in their native countries and cannot be exported. If you want to eat black mulberries, you have to pick them from the tree, or acquire them in jams and syrups. Humans are not the only ones to enjoy the fruit, of course; birds and animals, which are the main vehicles for dispersing mulberry seeds in their faeces, often get there first.

Leaves

The leaves of the black mulberry are usually very different to those of the white, being, as Gerard describes, 'broade and sharpe pointed; something harde, and nicked on the edges'. On old wood, as opposed to new shoots, they are broad, about 10 centimetres (4 in.) long and heart-shaped, with a pointed tip and serrated edges. Leaf shape is not always a reliable clue to identification, however. The leaves on new shoots, or new growth after pruning or pollarding, can be lobed or asymmetrically indented and resemble a fig leaf, fleur-de-lis or even a glove. They can be very different to the heart-shaped leaves on the rest of the tree and even look more like those of the white mulberry. While it can be disconcerting to see as many as a dozen different-shaped leaves on the same tree, flowering trees often have multiple leaf forms.

The feel and colour of the leaves, rather than just their shape, are better clues for identification. Black mulberry leaves are thick, the upper surface is coarse and the underside is noticeably hairy. Those of the white mulberry are thinner, lighter green, smoother and have a glossier, waxy surface. In winter, where both species are found, it can, however, be harder to tell whether a mulberry is white or black.

Origins

Black mulberries have been cultivated for so long that they are rarely found growing wild anywhere today, so it is uncertain where they originated. According to plant ecologist Peter Thomas they probably once grew as individual trees in temperate woodland and not in natural orchards, like apples or walnuts.[16] Oxford botanist Barrie Juniper,

Female flower of M. *nigra*. This will become the syncarp or cluster of tiny fruits we think of as the mulberry.

though, has suggested that mulberries (he doesn't say which species) may have been present in fruit forests in the Tianshan mountains alongside early apples, apricots, pears, figs and cherries.[17]

Today, black mulberries are most frequently associated with the area once covered by the Persian Sassanid Empire and the eastern Mediterranean, extending from Greece in the west to the Fergana Valley in what is now Tajikistan in the east. The species may still grow wild in northern Iran, on the shores of the Caspian Sea and in Colchis, an ancient region on the Black Sea south of the Caucasus Mountains. Colchis is where Jason, the leader of the Argonauts, travelled in search of the Golden Fleece – the winged ram Chrysomallos.[18]

Morus nigra leaves from the same tree.

It is not clear when the black mulberry first arrived in countries around the eastern Mediterranean, but it has certainly been known there since at least Roman times. Representations of mulberry trees and leaves were found in mosaics in villas in Pompeii, notably on the south wall of the House of Venus Marina, when they were excavated in 1859.[19] They had remained buried under volcanic ash since Mount Vesuvius erupted in 79 CE. Mineralized black mulberry seeds were also found in a sewer at the Roman town of Herculaneum, which suffered the same fate as Pompeii, offering evidence that the fruit was being eaten by ordinary citizens.[20] Pliny the Elder, who mentions mulberries several times in his writings, died in nearby Stabiae from the falling volcanic debris of the eruption while on a mission to rescue his friends Rectina and Pomponianus. Pliny's nephew, Gaius Plinius Caecilius Secundus (Pliny the Younger), wrote that he planted the garden of his villa in Laurentum, near Rome, with mulberry and fig trees.[21]

Varieties

Unlike the white mulberry, there is essentially only one species of black mulberry, *Morus nigra*, although there are a few different varieties, distinguished essentially by the shape and size of their fruit, which can range from 1 centimetre (0.4 in.) or so in length to 3 centimetres (1.2 in.) or more. The more common varieties are *Morus nigra* AGM (Royal Horticultural Society Award of Great Merit), Black Beauty, Chelsea (King James I), Jerusalem, Kaester and Noir of Spain.[22]

Pliny the Elder noticed this lack of diversity nearly 2,000 years ago, writing that the (black) mulberry had 'been neglected by the wit of man' – in other words, no hybrid varieties have been produced and few cultivars:

> In the case of this tree the devices of the growers have made the least improvement of any, and the mulberry of Ostia and that of Tivoli do not differ from that of Rome by named varieties or by grafting or in any other way except the size of the fruit.[23]

William Bean endorsed this, adding that it is 'a very unusual circumstance in a tree so long cultivated.'[24] Recent genetic analysis has shed some light on this. The black mulberry holds the world record for the number of chromosomes in its cells, having more (by far) than any other species of flowering plant. While most species of mulberry are genetically simple, with fourteen pairs of chromosomes, the black mulberry, M. *nigra*, has an astonishing 22 duplicate sets of these fourteen pairs of chromosomes (308 chromosomes in total). This is called 'polyploidy' and could explain why it is difficult for the species to produce new varieties, since even when a mutation occurs in one chromosome, it is over-ridden by other, nearly identical, chromosomes.

Horticulturalist Miles Hadfield has suggested that *Morus nigra* might even be a very early hybrid between two taxa of white mulberry, *Morus alba* and *Morus cathayana*, which once grew wild together in the mountains of central China. M. *cathayana* is also genetically complex, with five, six or eight sets of paired chromosomes and, says Hadfield, 'by hybridisation, the chromosome constituent may have built up into a new form, the complex 22 ploid black mulberry.'[25] More recently, Juniper has put forward some evidence to support the idea that the black mulberry may have evolved from mutations in a species of white mulberry.[26]

White Mulberry

The white mulberry is a more slender, upright tree than the black mulberry, as Gerard noted in his *Historie of Plants* in 1597: 'The white Mulberrie tree groweth until it come unto a great and goodly stature, almost as big as the [black]: the leaves are rounder, not so sharp pointed, nor so deeply snipt about the edges: the fruite is like the former, but that it is white and somewhat more tasting like wine.'[27] The buds of the white mulberry are light brown and the branches usually straight. The surface of the leaves has a waxed appearance.

Origins

Unlike the black mulberry, the white mulberry may still (rarely) be found growing wild – notably in the mountains of central and northern China, where it is known as *Sang shen* and in Japan, where it is

Male flowers are drooping catkins; female flowers resemble the mulberry fruit in shape. This is no. 33 in a series of fifty cigarette cards originally produced in 1924 by W. D. and H. O. Wills on 'Flowering Trees and Shrubs'. The artist is unknown.

called *kuwa* (桑). There, it is found as a scattered element of oak forests below 1,220 metres (4,000 ft), where it grows alongside the pagoda tree, walnut and juniper.[28]

The white mulberry naturally occurs in the broadleaved forests of the Upper Yangtze provinces and has been found in oases of the Xinjiang (or Taklamakan) Desert, where it probably grew alongside the black poplar and Siberian elm. *M. alba* may have been native to this area, or else have been introduced from the Kunlun Mountains to the south, or even from northwest China with the arrival of knowledge about silk farming. There are also reports of white mulberries growing wild in woodlands along the Kur, Araz and Samur rivers in Azerbaijan, but again these may also be introduced trees that have spread.

One of the rare accounts of white mulberry trees found growing in the wild – in virgin forest – comes from Commodore Matthew C. Perry of the United States Navy when, in 1853, he landed at Chichi-jima in the remote volcanic Ogasawara (Bonin) Islands, 1,000 kilometres (620 mi.) due south of Tokyo, during his expeditions to the China Seas and Japan:

> Dense forests of palm crowded up the hill-sides and into the ravines, and were of such close growth that their full development was hindered and other vegetation prevented. The fan-palm was the most abundant of the six species observed. Among the various trees was noticed a variety of the beech of considerable size, a large tree growing in abundance on the

Morus alba, Hyde Park Corner, London.

M. alba, part of the UK National Mulberry Collection in London.

mountains, which somewhat resembled the dog-wood, and an immense mulberry with an occasional girth of thirteen or fourteen feet.[29]

As it turns out, the mulberries that Perry found belong to a previously unknown species, albeit related to white mulberries, named *Ogasawara kuwa* in Japanese and given the Linnaean Latin name of *Morus boninensis*.[30] Some of the trees were already 2,800 years old at the time, based on a count of the annual rings of a stump found on one of the islands. The Ogasawara mulberry is only found on three islands: Otouto-jima, Chichi-jima and Haha-jima, and, because of uncontrolled logging, attempts to settle on the islands and a failed silk industry using introduced mulberry species, it has now entered

M. alba flowers in India, 2017.

the Japanese Red Data Book as 'critically endangered'.[31] In 2006 there were fewer than 170 surviving native trees in the islands.

According to Victor Hehn, there is no trace of the white mulberry ever growing in Europe before the fall of Constantinople in 1453.[32] Having been introduced in the late Middle Ages on the coat-tails of silk technology, probably from western Central Asia, the white mulberry followed the gradual spread of the silk industry from Asia to Europe, North and South America and parts of Africa. Of the different species, *Morus alba multicaulis*, or the 'many-stemmed mulberry', has become the preferred variety for sericulture almost everywhere. For sericulture, the large-leaved *M. multicaulis* (known as *Lu-sang* in China) is often grafted onto the strong trunk and root of *M. bombycis* to produce a low, shrubby tree with large, unlobed leaves.[33] *M. alba* has even become an invasive species in the U.S., where it hybridizes easily with the native red mulberry, threatening its survival as a species.[34]

Varieties

Compared to the black mulberry, a hallmark of the white mulberry is its greater diversity, as Serres noted in 1599: 'Of the white [mulberry], there is manifestly knowne three *species*, or sortes, distinguished by the onely colour of the fruit, which is white, blacke, and red.'[35] As we have seen, the colour of the fruit is not a good indicator of species and only certain white mulberry species, like *M. alba cathayana*, produce fruit that are actually white. It is not clear which three species Serres was referring to. The white fruit tastes very sweet, to the point of being insipid. Being much less juicy than black mulberries, they hold their shape and can be dried or even sold fresh in bulk. Some species of white mulberry, like *M. alba multicaulis*, produce purple-black fruit – firmer than that of the black mulberry, but with a similar, though less pronounced, tartness. Like the black mulberry, the leaves of the white mulberry are also very variable in form. They are usually glossy and hairless, but can be either lobed or simple, and tend to be more oval than the heart-shaped leaves of the black mulberry. As many as twenty different leaf forms have been found on a single tree.[36]

We now know that there are more than three species of white mulberry, with well over 1,100 different names for varieties, hybrids and cultivars. This is borne out by the British National Mulberry Collection, housed in the gardens of Buckingham Palace, which in 2014 contained 35 kinds of mulberry, divided into nine species and sub-species and including 24 cultivars, nearly all of them white mulberry.[37]

Of the fourteen trees in the Collection that were selected to be illustrated and described in a limited-edition book, *The Queen's Mulberries*, presented to Queen Elizabeth II on her Golden Jubilee in 2002, twelve are varieties or cultivars of white mulberry; the remaining two are the black mulberry and the paper mulberry.[38] Varieties of white mulberry in the Collection include the invitingly named 'Sugar

Drop' – a rare hybrid of the red and white mulberry – and the rather terrifyingly named 'Nuclear Blast', a dwarf hybrid that neither flowers nor fruits and has twisted leaves that even the most experienced mulberry amateur might be hard-pushed to identify as a *Morus*.

One characteristic of the white mulberry sets it apart not just from the black mulberry, but from all other species of plant. Something analogous to the sudden appearance of leaves described by Pliny happens when the male flowers (catkins) of the white mulberry release their pollen. Put simply, the part of the male catkin that produces and disperses pollen – the stamen and its pollen-bearing anther – is bent back under tension like a Roman catapult. The dry air of approaching spring causes threads retaining the bent stamen to tear, straightening it in less than 25 microseconds (millionths of a second), propelling the pollen into the atmosphere at half the speed of sound, or about 580 kph (350 mph).

This has earned the white mulberry the record for the fastest motion yet observed in biology, approaching the physical limits for

There are at least seventeen recognized species of white mulberry and hundreds of varieties and cultivars. The UK's National Mulberry Collection alone holds over thirty taxa.

Backlit leaves of *Morus alba*, showing the veins, north Texas, 2010.

movements in plants.[39] This phenomenon has the exotic name of 'explosive anther dehiscence' and has become the bane of allergy-sufferers across several states in the U.S., as visible clouds of mulberry pollen suddenly fill the air around the tree, to be carried on the wind.[40]

We will be returning to the white mulberry in more detail in the next chapter, where we look at the origins and early development of the relationship between mulberry and silk.

Red Mulberry

North America has its own native species, the red mulberry (*Morus rubra*), where it is found from northern Ontario (Canada) south to southern Florida and west to southeast South Dakota and central

RED MULBERRY

The red mulberry (*Morus rubra*) is endemic to North America and can grow to a great height. Illustration in Julia Ellen Rogers, *Trees* (1926).

Texas. Native Americans, including the Alabama, Cherokee, Comanche, Creek, Iroquois, Meskwaki, Muskogee, Natchez, Rappahannock, Seminole and Timucua, have long used it for food and medicinal purposes. For the Natchez, the red mulberry is associated with August, the sixth month of their lunar calendar, falling between the Peach month and the Great Corn month.

The red mulberry prefers deep, moist soils in forested floodplains and valleys, occurring in shady woods, along riverbanks and in ravines. The eighteenth-century explorer William Bartram frequently found red mulberries in forests of deciduous trees in Florida, South Carolina and Georgia, where they would be growing alongside magnolia, elm, oak, acer and other tall trees. He also occasionally found groves of cultivated red mulberries in abandoned Creek villages in the state of Georgia: 'These are always on the banks of rivers, swamps, the artificial mounds and terraces elevating them above the surrounding groves.' They were, he said, 'cultivated by the ancients on account of their fruit, as being wholesome and nourishing food.'[41]

The tallest of the mulberry species (although possibly equalled by *M. boninensis*, the Japanese Ogasawara Island mulberry), the red mulberry grows to a height of up to 18.3 metres (60 ft) and has a crown width of 12.2 metres (40 ft). Sometimes described as 'vase-shaped', its broad, rounded crown also makes it a useful shade tree. It was once common in Canada but is now a rare component of the Carolinian forest ecosystem of southern Ontario. There are only about 230 trees left in this area, in eighteen sites – mostly protected conservation areas, like Ball's Falls on the Niagara peninsula. Of these, only about 105 trees are considered to be mature.[42] Red mulberries have been felled to make way for urban development, but have also fallen victim to hybridization with introduced white mulberries, making it the most endangered tree species in Canada. In the U.S. the red mulberry is suffering a similar fate, where the white mulberry is also invasive. In a survey of flora of the New York Metropolitan Region by researchers at the Brooklyn Botanic Garden, while red mulberries had declined from twenty individuals in the period of 1901–50 to eight

Pierre-Joseph Redouté, *Morus rubra* (red mulberry), in Henri-Louis Duhamel du Monceau, *Traité des arbres et arbustes* (1809).

between 1951 and 2000, *M. alba* had increased from twenty to 81 in the same interval.[43]

In many ways *Morus rubra* resembles the white mulberry, with a similarly shaped leaf, which can be oval with a noticeably pointed tip, or lobed, rather like a fig leaf. However, while white mulberry leaves

M. rubra leaves turn a vivid yellow in autumn and some are lobed, Kew Gardens, London, 2018.

are light green and fine with a glossy upper surface, red mulberry leaves are darker green, highly textured, rough to the touch with hairs underneath and more matte. According to the nineteenth-century Scottish botanist John Claudius Loudon, red mulberry leaves 'are the worst of all the kinds of mulberry leaves for feeding silkworms'.[44]

The red mulberry usually has male and female flowers on the same tree (they are monoecious), but they can sometimes be on separate trees. The male flowers are drooping catkins 2.5–4 centimetres (1–1.6 in.) long, while the female catkins are about 2.5 centimetres long. Just like the white mulberry, the flowers are cross-pollinated by the wind. The female catkins develop into 'syncarps' that look rather like white or black mulberries, also made up of a number of single-seeded drupelets. As the 'berries' mature, they change colour from light green to red, and finally to a near-black. Rather like a cross between a white and a black mulberry, they are juicy and sweet. Unlike white and black mulberries, however, the red mulberry has never really travelled and does not thrive away from its native habitat. It seems to have made it to England around 1629 but has never been widely planted in Europe. William Jackson Bean, who spent his

The paper mulberry (*Broussonetia papyrifera*) is no longer classified as a *Morus* species. Kew Gardens, London, 2018.

working life at the Royal Botanic Gardens, Kew, as Head of the Arboretum and ultimately as Curator in the first part of the twentieth century, wrote of the red mulberry that 'at Kew it always has an unhappy appearance, and I do not know of good trees elsewhere.'[45]

Paper Mulberry

Finally, there is the paper mulberry, *Broussonetia papyrifera* (also known as *Morus papyrifera*), the bark of which has been used to make paper in China since around 100 CE and in Japan since about 600 CE. According to Loudon it is 'a deciduous, low tree or large shrub, a native of

China and Japan, and of the South Sea Islands'.[46] In fact, the species may have arrived in the Polynesian islands as part of the Austronesian migration from Taiwan and southern China. Bean says that he found it in some Dalmatian towns, especially at Spalato (Split), where it was planted as a street tree 'of neat, rounded shape'.[47] The wood is brittle, which makes the tree susceptible to breaking in high winds and can make it highly allergenic.

While remaining a genus of the *Moraceae* family, the paper mulberry has now been reclassified as *Broussonetia* and no longer belongs to the *Morus* genus, so is not strictly a mulberry. However, as Loudon explains, it 'so closely resembles the mulberry, that it was long considered to belong to that [*Morus*] genus, and still retains its English name of the paper mulberry'.

It certainly bears more than a superficial resemblance to mulberries, especially the white mulberry, with shiny leaves that can either be simple, heart-shaped and pointed with serrated margins, or lobed. They are, though, considered too rough to serve as food for silkworms.

Flowers of female paper mulberry, Freiburg Botanic Garden, Freiburg im Breisgau, Germany, 2011.

Loudon goes on to describe the fruit as 'oblong, of a dark scarlet colour when ripe, and of a sweetish, but rather insipid taste.'[48] Like true mulberries, they are syncarps, or aggregate fruit.

Bean describes two cultivars, *Cucullata*, which has boat-like leaves with upturned edges, and *Laciniata*, a dwarf variety with a tangle of slender leaves. 'Both the varieties here mentioned,' he writes, 'are merely curious freaks, but the type itself makes a handsome shrub; the male plant when freely furnished with its yellowish, drooping catkins is striking.'[49]

The paper mulberry readily colonizes areas where the soil has been disturbed (such as through farming or development) and can adapt to a wide variety of habitats. Trees are usually either male or female and where the two sexes are close enough for pollination, the fertile seeds are spread by birds and animals feeding on the fruit. The species can also propagate vegetatively, via its spreading roots. Because

Flowers of male paper mulberry, Fronton, France, 2014.

Fruit of the paper mulberry, Taiwan, 2004.

it is so successful as a colonizer, the paper mulberry has recently become the most invasive species in Pakistan. It was widely planted as a street tree when the new city of Islamabad was built in the 1960s, but its pollen has proven so highly allergenic that it is now being felled and replaced by more benign tree species.[50]

Having had a look at each of the main species of mulberry in their native lands, in the next chapter we will explore the origins of the intimate relationship between mulberry and silk and the beginnings of the tree's gradual globalization.

Bombyx mori on mulberry leaf, Cupertino, California, 2014.

two
Mulberries and Silk

❦

The white mulberry (*Morus alba*) and the silk moth (*Bombyx mori*) have been locked together in an eternal cycle ever since they first met. From a biological perspective, it looks like a one-way deal – the silk moth larvae ('silkworms') eat the leaves of the mulberry tree (their only source of food) and give nothing in return. But in hindsight it hasn't worked out too badly for the mulberry species. As joint shareholders in the global silk industry, mulberry trees now grow in parts of the world that their seeds would never have reached naturally.

About 4,700 years ago, starting with trial and error, the Chinese developed an integrated farming practice known as sericulture, involving the organized cultivation of mulberry trees (moriculture) to feed and rear silkworms, then harvesting their cocoons and reeling the silk thread, ready for weaving into textiles. The gradual development and dissemination of sericulture has been the main (but not the only) driving force behind the global migrations of the mulberry.

In this chapter we look at the way ancient civilizations in China and northern India first harnessed the natural miracle of silk. Over the course of the next four and a half millennia it became one of the most successful commodities the world has ever known, while the cultivation of mulberry trees for silk changed landscapes from China and Central Asia to Europe and the u.s.

The First Sericulturalist

The date is 2640 BCE, in the reign of the Yellow Emperor, Huangdi. On the forested slopes of China's Huang He (Yellow River) valley, the larvae of a wild species of moth, *Bombyx mandarina*, are feeding on white mulberry leaves as they have done since time immemorial, spinning their cocoons of raw silk every summer. Across the globe, in southern England, the massive standing stones of Stonehenge are being erected; Egypt's Great Pyramid of Giza has not yet been built, and the last woolly mammoths are still walking on Wrangel Island in the Arctic Ocean.

Around this time an ancient Chinese people were settling around the northern (Ordos) loop of the Yellow River, taking advantage of the well-watered, fertile soil for agriculture. Through a happy accident, they discovered *Bombyx mandarina*'s alchemical secret and harnessed it to weave the first silk fabric. In the following centuries, sericulture became so important for the Chinese people that they created a myth to explain its discovery – the myth of the first sericulturalist.[1]

In one version of this myth a young princess is described as sipping tea under a mulberry tree, when a silk cocoon falls into her hot drink and unwinds. But there were not really any 'princesses' then, and tea, which started out as a medicine, was not being drunk in this part of China at the time. Silk historian William Leggett offers a slightly different version of the myth, which we have abridged and embellished here.[2]

Huangdi's primary concubine, the beautiful fourteen-year-old Leizu (or Xi Lingshi), was walking among the white mulberry trees around the emperor's residence when she noticed a little caterpillar voraciously eating one of the leaves. Intensely curious by nature, she stopped to observe it. Fearing that the creature might harbour the spirit of a departed ancestor, she left it alone but went back every day, watching it grow bigger as it munched its way through countless mulberry leaves. After a few weeks, the creature – by now about

Bernhard Rode, *The Empress of China Culling the First Mulberry Leaves for Silk*, 1771, oil on canvas.

7 centimetres (3 in.) long – started to build a kind of web using thread from its mouth. It then used the same thread to shroud itself inside a pale-yellow cocoon. Believing the creature to have died, and still thinking it might be an ancestor, Leizu carried the cocoon to the imperial residence for safety. Five days later, a miracle happened – out of the shroud emerged a white, winged creature – the ancestor's spirit had been released! Caught by surprise, Leizu accidentally dropped the now empty cocoon into a bowl of hot water she was about to use to wash herself. In the hot water, the gum holding the cocoon together began to dissolve, allowing a long, loose thread to unwind. She plucked at the thread, but no matter how much she unravelled it, it never seemed to end. When she and one of her servants stretched the thread as far as it would go, it measured 1,200 paces (about 900 metres, or 0.5 mi.).

The Yangshao people, to whom Leizu belonged, were already skilled at weaving, so she was immediately able to see the potential

Silk thread and silkworm cocoons.

for this gleaming fibre. She asked her servants to gather as many cocoons as they could find, then boiled them and reeled the thread. This time, though, they did not wait for the moths to escape. When they had enough thread, they used it to weave a piece of silk cloth.

When it was finished, Leizu proudly showed the shimmering textile to the emperor – the first ever piece of silk fabric. He immediately realized that he was holding something very special and ordered the mulberry trees to be protected and the silk cocoons to be harvested and reeled every year. The world was on the cusp of a major cultural and economic revolution. Later, the Chinese people were so grateful for the prosperity that Leizu (the first sericulturalist) and Huangdi had brought them that they organized a festival in her honour, which was subsequently celebrated every year in 'silkworm month', the fourth month of the lunar calendar, at the start of the new silkworm season. Especially during the first millennium CE, the people erected statues and shrines to the Silkworm Goddess, as Leizu also became known.[3]

Mulberries and Silk

Today, over 4,500 years later, an estimated 626,000 hectares (1,547,000 ac) of the Chinese landscape are devoted to growing mulberry trees to support what is still the world's most important silk industry. In 1998, 432,820 tonnes of fresh silk cocoons were produced in China.[4] Despite the development of synthetic fibres in the late nineteenth century, global trade in cocoons of raw silk is still worth about U.S.$3.8 billion a year.[5]

Although Leizu is a legendary character, there is evidence to support the date of the late Neolithic era for the discovery of silk. Silk ribbons, threads and woven fragments found at Qianshanyang in Huzhou, Zhejiang province (about 100 kilometres, or 62 mi., due west of Shanghai), have been dated at about 2700 BCE. Furthermore, in 1927 a silkworm cocoon cut in half with a sharp tool was found at

Silk on sale in Beijing, China, today.

a Yangshao culture site on the Yellow River in Shanxi province, in northern China. It is thought to date from between 2600 and 2300 BCE and has been interpreted as evidence of at least a rudimentary silk industry.[6] If true, this would make sericulture the earliest known form of 'industrial' farming.[7] Subsequent research has shown that the cocoon was not from a *Bombyx* moth, though, but probably another wild species, such as *Rondotia menciana* Moore, which could mean that both wild and domesticated silkworms were being used in Neolithic and Shang silk production.[8]

Other archaeological finds suggest that the technique of silk making could have been discovered even earlier. A small, carved, ivory cup, believed to be between 6,000 and 7,000 years old (thus dating from about 4000 BCE), was unearthed at a Neolithic site in Zhejiang province and appears to show a silkworm design.[9] There is also evidence, as we shall see, that the Harappan people of the Indus Valley (modern Pakistan) may have been producing a non-mulberry kind of silk, using wild species of moth, from as early as the third millennium BCE, challenging the idea of a Chinese monopoly in this early period.[10]

Organic Alchemy

The ancient Chinese (and Harappan peoples) had discovered an organic alternative to the philosopher's stone, which was a mythical means to convert base metals into gold. Instead, they had found a way to turn a free, potentially inexhaustible supply of simple plant matter (mulberry leaves) into a precious commodity (silk). And when trade in silk reached its most lucrative point, it really was worth its weight in gold.

The silkworm's organic alchemy starts even before it munches on the leaves of the mulberry. Chemical compounds in the plant first attract the silkworm to the leaf, then trigger a biting reflex and finally make it swallow. But here the plot takes a fascinating twist. The stem and leaves of all species of mulberry contain a milky latex that is fatal to most herbivorous insects – except the larvae of both the wild and domesticated silk moth.[11] This sap contains active compounds (alkaloids), which, when ingested, block the ability of insect larvae to break down and use the sugars in the mulberry leaf, effectively causing them to starve to death.[12] The silkworm has developed a way around this, however, and will thrive on mulberry leaves while other caterpillars eating them will shrivel and die. Interestingly, this same defensive process makes the active compounds in mulberry latex useful in reducing blood sugar levels in humans with Type 2 diabetes.

After mating, the female silk moth lays between three and five hundred tiny, fertilized white eggs (sometimes called 'grains' or 'seeds') on the mulberry leaves, twigs and discarded parts of its own cocoon. Each egg is about 1 millimetre (0.04 in.) in length. In the wild, the eggs would be laid in late summer or early autumn and remain dormant over the winter, but in modern sericulture they are kept refrigerated until required the following year. When the eggs hatch the following spring, the silkworms are at first hairy and about 3 millimetres (0.1 in.) in length, earning them the nickname 'ants'. These tiny larvae can only eat the first, tender mulberry leaves, so hatching has to be timed precisely to coincide with the opening of the mulberry buds.

In sericulture, it is a delicate art to synchronize hatching of the eggs with the supply of fresh mulberry leaves – and this is not without stress for the producers. If the eggs hatch too early the 'ants' will starve, as there will be no leaves to feed on. Too late and the hatchlings will be unable to bite into and digest the tougher, fully developed leaves. Careful preparation is essential.

Wisdom regarding best practices in moriculture and sericulture came to be written down in various Chinese texts, at least as early as the thirteenth century CE.[13] Some sixteenth- and seventeenth-century Chinese texts on the subject were translated into French and Italian and later formed the basis for manuals in English in the seventeenth century.[14] But there was also an accumulation of folk wisdom, which gives a colourful insight into the fragile business of rearing silkworms. According to the *Countrey Farme*, an English translation (with Anglicized authors' names) of a sixteenth-century French manual, *La Maison*

Jan van der Straet (Joannes Stradanus), 'The Gathering of Mulberry Leaves and the Feeding of the Silkworms', c. 1595, engraving on antique laid paper. Plate no. 5 from a series of six published as *Vermis Sericus*, illustrating the history and techniques of silk production.

Rustique: 'The carefull Huswife, so soone as the Spring draweth neere, and that she shall see that the Mulberrie-tree beginneth to bud, shall make in readinesse egges of Wormes, which shee hath kept all the Winter before, to be brooded and sit upon.'[15]

In traditional European rural silk-making communities, women used to carry the eggs in pouches next to their bosom as spring approached – a form of low-tech incubation – in order to get the timing right, as the *Countrey Farme* recommends:

> The meanes to make them breed, is, after that you have watered and bathed them with white Wine, rather than warme water, to lay them neere the fire, untill they be a little warmed: then to lay them betwixt two pillowes stuffed with feathers, and made likewise somewhat warme, or betwixt the breasts of women (provided that they have not their termes at that time).[16]

For the next 45 days or so after hatching, the silkworm eats voraciously, growing to an astonishing 10,000 times its original size – up to about 7.5 centimetres (3 in.) in length. During this time, it sheds its skin five times, each moulting called an 'instar'. Over the spring and early summer, the mulberry leaves also grow in size as the silkworm develops, reaching lengths of up to 20 centimetres (8 in.) and widths of 10 centimetres (4 in.) in some species.

According to a seventeenth-century text on sericulture by the French expert Jean-Baptiste Letellier, published in English by William Stallenge, 'silkworms should always be fed leaves of their own age, young caterpillars fed tender young leaves, older caterpillars larger and tougher leaves.'[17] When this is not possible, the leaves are shredded, first into small pieces and then increasingly coarsely as the silkworms grow.

Even in fairly recent times, traditional rural sericulturalists would pamper their silkworms like royalty, believing that they could be put off their food by the wrong smells, or even loud noises, like thunder. If that happened, the precious harvest of silk cocoons would fail and the farmers' income would be lost for that year. The *Countrey Farme* gives this a slight twist, recommending that the tiny silkworms be offered some of the domestic odours that might comfort a sixteenth-century French farmer:

> These little beasts may not be touched with your hands but as little as may be: for the more they are handled, the more they are hindered thereby, because they are verie exceeding tender and daintie, especially at such time as they doe cast, or change. And yet notwithstanding, they must bee kept verie cleane and neat, and all their little dung taken from them everie three daies. The place must likewise be perfumed with Frankincense, Garlicke, Onions, Larde, or broyled Sawsages, that you may minister matter of pleasure unto these little creatures and againe, if they be weake and sicke, these smells refresh and recover them againe.[18]

After its fifth 'instar', the silkworm somehow knows it is time to move on in life and become a moth – as we will see. Over the next 48 hours, the silkworm uses special glands in its mouthparts to produce the silk fibre, first spinning a loose web to anchor it to a (mulberry) twig and then weaving a complex cocoon, making nearly a kilometre (0.6 mi.) of thread. Individual silk fibres consist of a protein (*fibroin*), surrounded by a sticky gum coating called sericin, as we have seen. This gum helps the fibres to stick together into an exceptionally strong, elastic thread.

Inside the cocoon the process of metamorphosis begins. The silkworm changes, first to a chrysalis (*pupa*) and then, about three weeks later, into an adult (*imago*) before hatching. In Chinese sericulture, the cocoons would be harvested after about eight days, before the chrysalis had turned into the *imago*, or moth-to-be.

Centuries of selective breeding have had a dramatic impact on the once free-roaming, wild *Bombyx mandarina*. It has now mutated into *Bombyx mori*, a blind, flightless and almost colourless insect that can no longer survive without human intervention.[19] The domesticated silk moth has wings, but cannot fly. It has mouthparts, but in its short lifetime as an adult (about a week), it does not eat. The silkworm itself can barely walk.

Particularly tragic for *Bombyx mori* is that domestication has also affected the moth's sensitivity to environmental odours to such an extent that it has trouble finding the mulberry leaves on which to lay its eggs.[20] Happily though, this hasn't affected its ability to mate, which is also governed by olfaction. A male *Bombyx mori* moth, like its wild ancestor, can still detect a few molecules of the female sex pheromone, *bomykol*, several kilometres away.[21] (Not that it helps them much, however, as, lacking flight, the pair depend on human breeders to bring them together.) *Bomykol*, which in 1959 was the first pheromone to be described chemically, is still able to trigger the mating act itself, though, so all is not lost.

Recent genetic analysis has shown that the relationship between mulberry and silkworm is even more intimate than was ever imagined:

fragments of mulberry plant genetic material have somehow become incorporated into the silkworm itself.[22] So-called micro-RNA molecules (miRNAs) of the mulberry have been found in tissue cells in the silkworm's silk glands.[23] In the mulberry tree these molecules signal leaf ageing, but in the silkworm they probably tell the larva that it's time to start spinning its cocoon. Other mulberry miRNAs have been found in the silkworm, too, which probably help synchronize the timing of the larva's development with that of the leaves it feeds on – which seems to be critical for the silkworm's survival.

The Secret of Chinese Silk

Little is known for sure about the development and spread of sericulture during its first 2,500 years and most of our evidence comes from archaeological studies, which are of course subject to interpretation. By the time of the Shang dynasty (1600–1046 BCE) however, sericulture seems to have been well established in the region around the Yellow River known as the Ordos Loop. The Shang people are credited with some of the earliest forms of writing – inscribed on so-called 'oracle bones' or 'dragon bones', which were used for divination. These were often the shoulder bones of oxen or the plastrons (flat undersides) of turtle shells, onto which a question, for example about the silk cocoon harvest, would be scratched. A hole would then be drilled into the bone and a heated metal spike pushed into it, causing the bone to crack. A soothsayer would interpret the fracture lines to answer the question.

Oracle bones dating from the Shang dynasty found at Gaoyang in Hebei province (*hebei* means 'north of the river') appear to describe silk-making techniques.[24] Characters on these bones appear to show mulberry trees and silkworms, as well as methods of twisting and reeling silk thread.[25] Further evidence for sericulture in ancient China comes from a piece of turtle plastron dating from the second millennium BCE, which has been interpreted as showing a hand holding a five-lobed leaf of the white mulberry, *M. alba*.

Four dots depict silkworm eggs – probably the eggs of the wild silk moth *Bombyx mandarina*.[26]

While there is little doubt that sericulture first arose in Neolithic China, silk fibres also dating from the third millennium BCE have been found in a bangle and wire necklace recovered from an archaeological site in the Indus Valley (Pakistan and northern India), and linked to the Harappan culture of this region.[27] This silk thread comes from species of wild moth indigenous to South Asia, *Antheraea assamensis* and *A. mylitta*, and not the domesticated silk moth *Bombyx mori*, or its probable ancestor, *B. mandarina*, used in Chinese sericulture. *Antheraea* moth species feed on the leaves of forest trees, such as oak, birch, beech, maple, walnut and some fruit trees. Unlike *Bombyx mori*, *Antheraea* moths can still survive in the wild.

This wild or 'tussah' silk is different to silk produced by *Bombyx* moths in several important respects. What was to make Chinese silk so highly valued is that the sericin gum coating of the fibre was first removed by boiling the cocoons. This made it possible to reel off the long, unbroken fibres and to twist them together to make a stronger thread. When this is woven it results in very fine silk cloth, with a unique and highly prized lustre.

In contrast, tussah silk was originally derived using cocoons from which the silk moth had already escaped, either by biting its way out or through a natural hole. Tussah silk had to be spun (rather than reeled), using broken threads from which the sericin coating had not been boiled off. This produced a coarser fibre, which never acquired the lustre of reeled, boiled silk – although it had a texture and natural honey colour that made (and still makes) it sought-after in its own right.[28]

An important collateral consequence of Chinese reeled silk is that the moth is killed inside the cocoon during the boiling process – and was (and is still is) fried and eaten as a delicacy once the thread has been reeled. Hindu scriptures forbid the taking of life, so whole cocoons with unbroken threads could not be used. Thus, when Buddhist cultures in Central and Southern Asia later learned

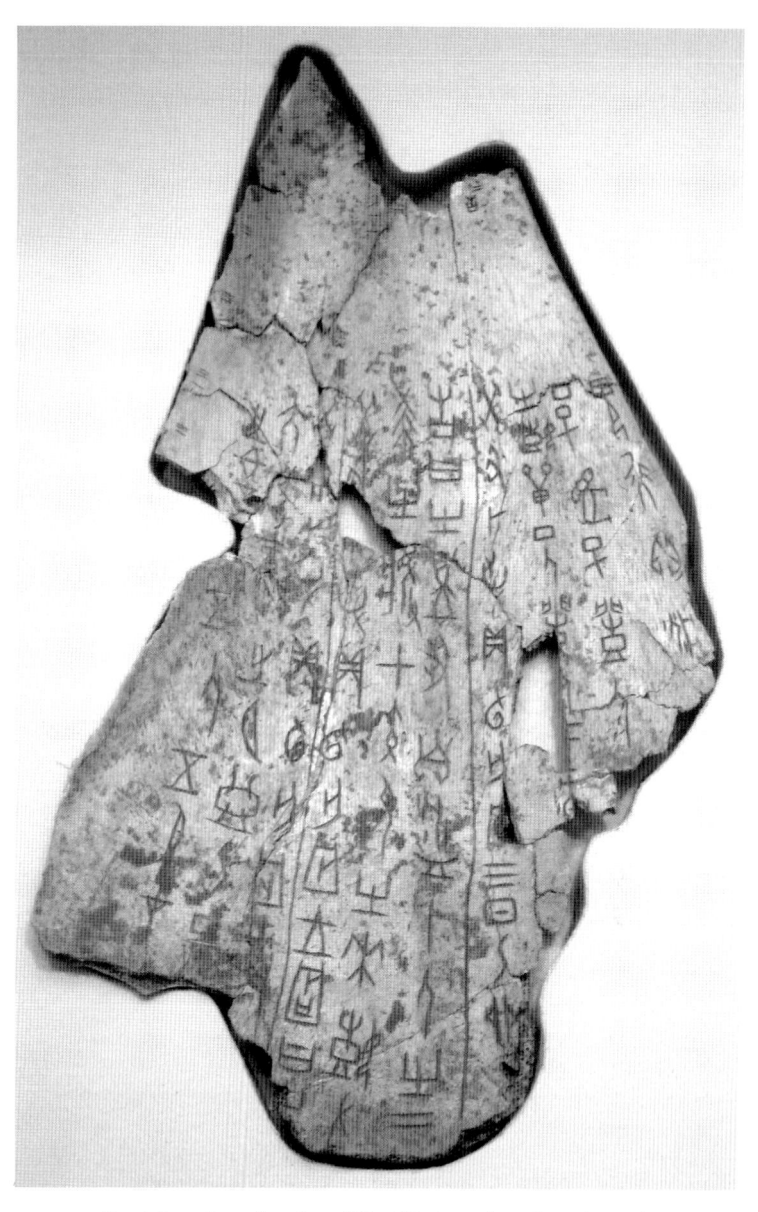

Oracle bone from the reign of King Wu Ding (late Shang dynasty), c. 1200 BCE. Some bones relate to sericulture.

Large bronze wine jar with pictorial decoration (*Fangu*), Eastern Zhou dynasty, Warring States period, 5th–4th century BCE, showing women picking mulberry leaves (bottom panel). They are using hooks and baskets like those still in use 1,000 years later.

the Chinese techniques of sericulture using *Bombyx mori* and mulberry leaves, they instead developed their own version of the Harrappan method, forgoing the fine silks of the Chinese in order to facilitate the silk moth's escape.

The real secret of Chinese silk, then, was not that silk was produced by the larvae of a moth – a process which nonetheless continued to elude civilizations around the eastern Mediterranean and Caspian Sea until as late as the sixth century CE – but the technology of sericulture based on a unique combination of mulberry leaves, *Bombyx mori* silkworms and the boiling and reeling of whole cocoons containing live moths.[29]

Moriculture

By 2000–1100 BCE, the early peoples in China were already cultivating the native *M. alba* to support the production of silk. Zhou period (1046–256 BCE) folk songs made frequent reference to silk weaving and textiles,[30] and, as early as 594 BCE, moriculture – the organized cultivation of mulberry trees as part of the production of silk cocoons – was so well established that the emperor levied a tax on inherited mulberry fields, which the farmers paid in hemp, grain and silk.[31]

The mulberry trees in these fields were probably not yet being coppiced (pruned near to ground level), but were instead left to grow, and would have been a native, possibly wild, species of *Morus alba*. Bronze urns from the Warring States period (476–225 BCE) clearly show women climbing into mulberry trees and picking the leaves, using a 'mulberry hook'.[32] On one of these urns, a basket is depicted hanging from a branch of a tree to hold the leaves. Both the hook and the basket are very similar to implements portrayed in Chinese illustrations from the fourteenth century CE and were evidently still in use at that time.

It is often said that the Chinese kept the technology of sericulture a closely guarded secret, with severe punishments for those who leaked their methods, or exported silkworms, silk moth eggs, mulberry saplings or seeds.[33] But according to Silk Road scholar Susan Whitfield, 'only remnants of the law code of the early period survive and there is nothing mentioning silk in the extant sections on the materials that were forbidden for export.'[34] It is possible, though, that a growing sense of unified national identity, together with pride in their sericulture skills, may have made Chinese peasants keen to keep control of the production of fine silk. Added to this was a sense of loyalty to the emperor and his family, who ultimately held the monopoly over silk and silk technology.[35] There was also, of course, the geographical isolation of China, shielded by perilous mountains to the west and vast deserts to the north.

Whether or not there was deliberate withholding, the technique of Chinese sericulture travelled much more slowly than the fabric itself. Long before organized trade, silk was probably being bartered and offered as gifts in diplomatic attempts to maintain peace, especially with sometimes hostile, largely pastoralist, steppe neighbours to the north.[36] Some silk was undoubtedly carried off in raids – Chinese silk from the fourth and fifth centuries BCE has been found in Pazyryk, Siberia, far beyond the northern borders where it may have been offered as a gift.[37]

Hostilities with the steppe peoples may also have been one of the reasons that large numbers of northern Chinese migrated to the

Harvesting mulberry leaves (*sang-chi*), 14th-century woodcut illustration, China.

Korean peninsula in the second century BCE. The migrants, some of them skilled in sericulture, also took with them *Bombyx mori* eggs and the techniques of rearing silkworms, harvesting and boiling the cocoons and reeling and weaving the silk thread. This region has native species of white mulberry, including *Morus alba* and *M. notabilis*, so it was a relatively easy matter to establish sericulture there. By the third century CE sericulture had travelled on to neighbouring Japan, where species of white mulberry were also endemic.

Westward Spread of Sericulture

Knowledge of the techniques of Chinese sericulture spread west to Central Asia long before it eventually reached Constantinople in the sixth century CE, following the westward expansion of trade in silk. According to a widely held but oversimplified account, knowledge of Chinese silk only began to seep westwards out of China during the former Han dynasty (140–134 BCE), when Emperor Wudi sent his envoy Zhang Qian to form an alliance with the Yuezhi peoples, who had been pushed out of their steppe homelands. The Yuezhi, who were skilled at horsemanship (like their nemesis the Xiongnu), had settled in Bactria (present-day Uzbekistan). The northern Chinese wanted the tough, fast horses of the Fergana Valley, while the steppe peoples were keen to acquire the brightly coloured, exotic silk textiles – especially quilted silk, which was warm, yet light. Rare silk clothing was a way to signal status and to set oneself apart from one's rivals, who would be dressed in locally produced leathers, felts and furs.

It took Zhang Qian thirteen years before he returned, having been taken prisoner by the Xiongnu. He failed to make a deal with the Yuezhi but did bring back invaluable information about the advanced state of civilization in Bactria. This helped to stimulate trade, not just in silk, but in many other commodities. This in turn reinforced the diffuse network of tracks that had already been in existence throughout Central Asia for centuries – what later became known as 'the Silk Road' (a term only coined in the nineteenth century by a

German traveller and scientist, Baron Ferdinand von Richthofen, as *Seidenstrasse*).[38] Rather than being a region of transition, through which traders passed on their way to the west, Central Asia was, as Susan Whitfield has put it, more like a 'great sea' with 'numerous currents in complex interaction'.[39]

The first evidence of mulberry-based sericulture west of China was in the kingdom of Khotan on the southern edge of the Taklamakan Desert in the Tarim Basin, sometime between 150 and 350 CE. This transmission of knowledge may have been part of a diplomatic gesture by the Han imperial court, in the form of a marriage alliance with the Khotanese royal family. But a celebrated legend passed down to us describes it as an act of treachery.

According to the legend, a beautiful Chinese princess was betrothed to the king of Khotan. Eager to acquire the 'secret of silk', he told his future bride that, if she wished to continue to wear silk, she would have to bring the wherewithal to make it. Khotan, he said, had neither mulberries nor silkworms. But, the legend insists, to take them out of China was forbidden.

The Hungarian-born archaeologist Sir Aurel Stein, who excavated ancient sites in Khotan from 1900, relates the legend, as told

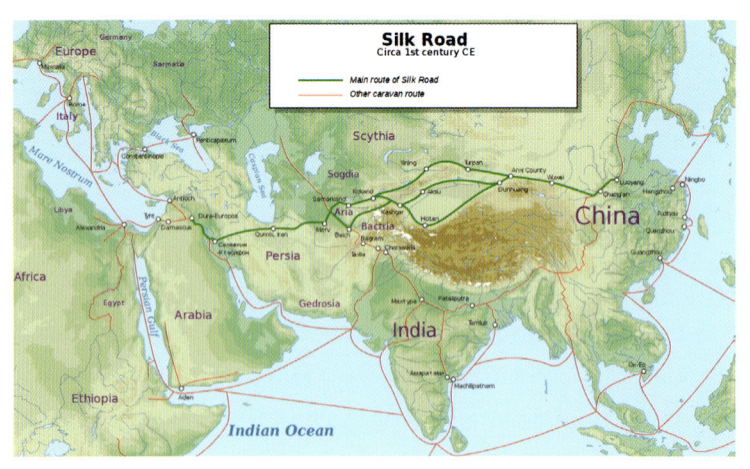

The 'Silk Road' in the 1st century CE. The 'road' was really a network through which much more than silk travelled, including ideas, religions, as well as commodities, gold and gemstones.

Mulberries and Silk

Rectangular votive panel, 7th–8th century CE, illustrating, on one side, the legend of the introduction of sericulture to the regions of Khotan. The central figure is a Chinese princess who smuggled mulberry seeds and eggs of the silk moth to Khotan, hiding them in her headdress.

in the sixteenth-century account of a pilgrimage to the west (*Xiyouji*) made by a seventh-century Buddhist monk, Xuanzang:[40]

> When this request [for the hand of the princess in marriage] had been acceded to, [the king] dispatched an envoy to escort the princess from China, taking care to let the future queen know through him that, in order to assure herself of fine silk robes when in Khotan, she had better bring some mulberry seeds and silkworms with her.
>
> The princess, thus advised, secretly procured mulberry seeds and silkworms' eggs, and by concealing them in the lining of her headdress, which the chief of the frontier guards did not dare to examine, managed to remove them safely to Khotan. On her first arrival and before her solemn entry into the royal palace, she stopped at the site where subsequently the Lu-she convent was built, and there left the silkworms and the mulberry seeds. From the latter grew up the first mulberry trees, with the leaves of which the silkworms were fed when their time had come.[41]

This story is beautifully told in a painted wooden votive panel that Stein retrieved from Dandan-Uiliq (130 kilometres northeast of Khotan), dated to the seventh–eighth century CE, and now in the British Museum. Stein found the dried-out trunks of rows of mulberry trees sticking up out of the desert sand that had engulfed the

Dessicated remains of mulberry trees found in Niya, in the Taklamakan Desert (Khotan), by Sir Aurel Stein on his archaeological expedition in 1907.

site he excavated in the former oasis of Niya. He also found poplars and evidence of fruit trees, showing how abundant the oasis vegetation had once been, thanks to irrigation 'tanks' (shallow reservoirs) – some of which still held water.

In reality, it would have taken several years for mulberry trees grown from seed to produce enough leaves to feed the thousands of silkworms needed to make even one silk tunic. But species related to the white mulberry, including *M. macroura*, *M. mongolica* and *M. serrata*, are native to Tibet, the Himalayas and Mongolia and could have been propagated as 'truncheons' or planted as saplings. The silkworm eggs would have been less of an issue as they are so tiny that the princess could have easily concealed tens of thousands in her headdress, ready to hatch in the spring.

The Taklamakan Desert is a forbidding place with high, drifting dunes, and it has claimed many lives. Its name may come from the Persian *tark* to abandon and *makan*, meaning 'place' ('the place of no return', or, in Turki, *aqlar makan*: 'go in and you won't come out', an allusion to its desolate, arid conditions).[42] But a series of rivers that disappeared underground created fertile oases suitable for growing fruit trees – including mulberries. Khotan went on to become a highly successful centre for the production of silk and was well placed for trade east, towards China, and to the west. The Taklamakan was historically skirted on its northern and southern extremes by established routes, in use since at least the second millennium BCE, notably to carry nephrite jade to China from mines in the Kunlun Mountains to the south.

During the Han dynasty (260 BCE–220 CE), while trade in silk was in its infancy, the shimmering fabric had already become a currency in its own right. Silk was even used to pay soldiers' wages, while itinerant Buddhist monks used silks for offerings in temples, as well as to pay their way. Merchants and other travellers would also carry bolts of silk to exchange for goods and services.[43]

Mixing Mulberry Species

A century or two after sericulture and moriculture became established in Khotan, where it was based on white mulberry species, the technology reached the Fergana Valley and the ancient civilizations of Bactria and Sogdia, which straddled today's Uzbekistan, southern Kyrgyzstan and Tajikistan. The city state of Samarkand (now in Uzbekistan) was to become a major hub for trade on the Silk Road, most notably with the Persian Sassanid Empire, from about 260 CE until it came to an end with the Muslim conquest of 651 CE.

It is likely that, as sericulture developed here, *Bombyx* silkworms were first fed on native *M. nigra*, black mulberries. The Fergana Valley marks the eastern limit of the natural range of *M. nigra* and offers a natural east–west corridor. It would have been easy to carry enough tiny silkworm eggs from Khotan or China to bootstrap the practice of sericulture, but the availability of white mulberry leaves would have been more of an obstacle, albeit surmountable. The Pamir mountain range to the east presents a natural topographical barrier to the east of the Tarim Basin and also probably marks the eastern limit of the range of M. *alba*. The mulberry propagates both through seeds in its fruit, which are excreted by birds and other animals that feed on them, and vegetatively, by layering. High mountain ranges would present an impediment to both, so it is likely that when M. *alba* was introduced to the east of the Pamirs it was brought by travellers along the Silk Road, as part of an effort to improve the yield of cocoons from silkworms already being raised on M. *nigra*.

Silkworms fed on the leaves of M. *alba* grow faster than those fed on M. *nigra* and produce finer silk, in greater quantities. This would have been obvious to anyone who had the opportunity to compare the yields from silkworms fed on the two species of mulberry. The advantages of using M. *alba* would have been clear enough for producers gradually to abandon M. *nigra* in favour of the introduced white mulberry for sericulture. Today, sericulture still thrives in the region, but is based on M. *alba*.

Sericulture in the Empires of the West

Silk had been known in the region around the eastern Mediterranean and Caspian Sea since antiquity, and by the first century of the Christian era was already a highly valued commodity. Under Tiberius (14–37 CE), the Roman Senate even passed sumptuary laws forbidding men to 'defile themselves' by wearing silk.[44] But how silk was produced – and exactly where it came from – remained a mystery.

Some scholars claim that the ancient Greeks knew not only about silk and silk weaving but about sericulture as early as the fifth or sixth century BCE, but that attempts to trace this in the literature have failed because the Greek word for silk (*seres*) was not yet being used.[45] There are, though, references to '*amorgís*', a diaphanous form of linen, which was woven from threads 'hackled' from the bark of trees.[46] Ezekiel, writing in exile in Babylon in the sixth century BCE, may have been referring to this *amorgís* (silk) when he described a young woman (as it transpires, a prostitute) dressed in 'fine linen and costly fabric

Chinese jin-silk panel, featuring a lion, camel and elephant, a deity and a human figure. Possibly representing a Persian merchant on the Silk Road stopping at an oasis, with the figures reflected in the water. Northern dynasties (365–581 CE).

and embroidered cloth' (Ezekiel 16:13).[47] The 'hackled' stuff could also have referred to discarded silkworm cocoons still attached to the trees after the silk moths had hatched. It could also have been the tussah silk that had been produced in northern India since the third millennium BCE, as we have seen above.

Aristotle (384–322 BCE) apparently had some knowledge of the silkworm and, according to his *History of Animals*, was aware that at one point in its development it became encased inside a kind of spider's web, where it turned into a chrysalis and finally emerged as a winged creature, casting off the 'tunic' it had been wearing.[48] Again, it is likely that he had seen, or had heard about, the wild 'tussah' silk moth. As it happens, no one in the empire was very interested, and the information was not followed up for several generations.

Roman natural philosopher Pliny the Elder also knew that silk was produced by a caterpillar, but thought the insect rubbed it off the surface of leaves:

At first they [the caterpillars] assume the appearance of small butterflies with naked bodies, but soon after, being unable to endure the cold, they throw out bristly hairs, and assume quite a thick coat against the winter, by rubbing off the down that covers the leaves, by the aid of the roughness of their feet. This they compress into balls by carding it with their claws, and then draw it out and hang it between the branches of the trees, making it fine by combing it out as it were: last of all, they take and roll it round their body, thus forming a nest in which they are enveloped.[49]

And, although this may refer to tussah silk, not mulberry silk:

The Chinese . . . are famous for the woollen substance obtained from their forests; after a soaking in water, they comb off the white down of the leaves, and so supply our women with the double task of unravelling the threads and weaving them together again.[50]

Harvesting mulberry leaves. A mulberry hook leans against the tree on the right. This 19th-century Western engraving shows men gathering the leaves, but it was usually women's work in China.

Fifty years earlier, the Roman poet Virgil (70–19 BCE) wrote of silk – or was it linen – in his *Georgics* (Book II):

Quid numera Aethiopum molli canentia lana;
Vellera que ut foliis depicta et tennia Seres

This is nothing but white wool from Ethiopian trees;
a duvet, harvested from the leaves of trees in Seres

Seres was the name the Greeks had given to the Chinese, hence *sericulture*.

Pliny's 'unravelling' and 'reweaving' may refer to the work of women weavers on the island of Kos, who were known to unravel plain silks and weave them again in a different way. According to a French Roman Catholic priest, Abbé Brottier, writing around 1842, the Romans knew of three kinds of silk: silk from Seres (China), silk from Assyria and silk from Kos.[51] The silk from Kos was used for men's clothing, but the finer silk for women came from Assyria ('Assyria tamen bombyce feminis cedimus').

Abbé Brottier may have been referring to another text by Pliny, in which he shows some awareness of the silkworm and how it produces silk thread:

> in the Ile of Cthos there growe Cypress trees, Turpentine trees, Ashes, and Oakes; of the leaves of which trees, fallen to the ground in maturity, through humidity of the same, breede wormes bringing forth silke. That in Assyria the Sylkeworme called by the Greekes and Latines, Bombyx, makes his nest upon the earth, which he fastens to the stones, where it hardeneth very much, remaining there conserved all the yeere, that makes webs after the fashion of Spiders.[52]

Similarly, Pausanias, a Greek traveller and geographer living in the second century (110–180 CE), writing a few years after Pliny, took the silkworm to be a worm 'about twice the size of a scarab beetle, and having eight legs like a spider, living for five years, at the end of which it dies of indigestion, with its stomach filled with fine thread [*ser*]'.[53]

The Romans had been trading indirectly with India since the first century CE, mostly via maritime routes from southern India to the Red Sea that had been developed by the Aksumite Empire in what is now northern Ethiopia and Eritrea. The Aksumites acted as key intermediaries, having created their own currency, which facilitated this trade. Trade was not only in (mostly Chinese) silk, but glass, spices, ivory, cotton and other items. Incomplete knowledge of how silk was made may have filtered back to Rome along these routes, too, but not in a way that allowed sericulture to be developed.

These eastern maritime routes became much more developed after the Roman Empire segued into the Byzantine Empire (or Eastern Roman Empire), between the fourth and sixth centuries CE and the capital moved from Rome to Constantinople (modern-day Istanbul).

To help satisfy their demand for silk, the Romans set up a successful silk-weaving industry of their own, using Chinese yarn and centred on the cities of Beirut and Tyre.[54] If supplies were short, the weavers would unpick and reweave Chinese silk fabric, as we have seen. Roman weavers – particularly those on the island of Kos – were greatly admired for their skill. The resulting material would then be sent to Syria to be dyed. A special feature of Roman (and later Byzantine) silk was the coveted purple dye, obtained from murex shellfish found only in the eastern Mediterranean – which was already being used in the time of the Phoenicians (1500 BCE–300 BCE), an ancient civilization occupying a region that roughly corresponded to modern-day Lebanon and parts of Israel and Syria. The Phoenicians were skilled merchants and traders and colonized lands around the Mediterranean, notably in the first millennium CE.

Constantinople and the Smuggler Monks

In 330 CE Constantine the Great shifted the capital of the Roman Empire eastwards to the ancient settlement of Byzantium on the Bosphorus, renaming it Constantinople. When Justinian I became ruler of the Byzantine Empire in 527 CE, the Sassanid Empire still held tight control on trade in silk fabric and thread from China, whether it arrived overland or by sea via India. The Byzantine and Sassanid empires, which shared several borders, used diplomatic means to avoid conflict and keep trade open. As silk was such an economically important part of all their trade, its supply played a key role in relations between the two empires. But the Sassanids exploited their monopoly over the supply of silk to the Byzantine Empire by imposing high tariffs.

Justinian sought to develop alternative supply routes, bypassing the Sassanid monopoly altogether, despite tight trade agreements that had been drafted to calm tensions between the warring rivals. This included a failed attempt to deal directly with the Aksumites, who were also trading with India. But the real *coup de grâce* would be to acquire the secret of sericulture itself – the ability to make silk, rather than just weave and dye it. With black mulberry leaves already abundant across the Byzantine Empire, what was missing was the silkworm and an understanding of how silk thread was produced and harvested.

The only contemporary account of how Justinian acquired this esoteric and crucial technology comes from the Roman historian Procopius, who documented Justinian's reign (in sometimes unflattering detail). Born in Caesarea – modern-day Palestine – Procopius writes:

> About the same time there came from India certain monks; and when they had satisfied Justinian Augustus that the Romans no longer should buy silk from the [Sassanid] Persians, they promised the emperor in an interview that they

would provide the materials for making silk so that never should the Romans seek business of this kind from their enemy the Persians, or from any other people whatsoever. They said that they were formerly in Serinda, which they call the region frequented by the people of the Indies, and there they learned perfectly the art of making silk. Moreover, to the emperor who plied them with many questions as to whether he might have the secret, the monks replied that certain worms were manufacturers of silk, nature itself forcing them to keep always at work; the worms could certainly not be brought here alive, but they could be grown easily and without difficulty; the eggs of single hatchings are innumerable; as soon as they are laid men cover them with dung and keep them warm for as long as it is necessary so that they produce insects. When they had announced these tidings, led on by liberal promises of the emperor to prove the fact, they returned to India. When they had brought the eggs to Byzantium, the method having been learned, as I have said, they changed them by metamorphosis into worms which feed on the leaves of mulberry. Thus began the art of making silk from that time on in the Roman Empire.[55]

In oft-repeated versions of this account, the monks were two 'Nestorians' who smuggled silkworm eggs into Constantinople from Serinda, hidden in hollowed-out sticks. Serinda may have been Serindia, which is to say Khotan, or somewhere in Central Asia like Bactria, although this is disputed. Nestorian Christians (more generally called the 'Church of the East') were a breakaway sect formed around 500 CE, following a theological schism in the Byzantine Empire. Fleeing persecution by 'Orthodox' Christians who challenged their views, they first settled in Persia, but continued to migrate eastwards, making new converts to Christianity along the way.

Nestorian monks eventually established monasteries and settlements as far north as Mongolia. With connections along the Silk

Workers at the UK's Lullingstone silk farm in Kent harvested mulberry leaves in the 20th century using the same methods as those who lived 2,000 years ago.

Road all the way to China, this Nestorian network offered an ideal vehicle for short-circuiting the whole silk supply chain, with its gateway to the Byzantine Empire still rooted in Sassanid Persia. As just 1 ounce (28 g) of *Bombyx mori* 'seed' contains something like 16,000 eggs, it is plausible that the monks could have brought enough with them in hollow sticks to bootstrap at least a cottage silk industry. Around 5,500 silkworms are needed to make 1 kilogram of raw silk – and about 100 kilograms of mulberry leaves to feed them. As there is no record of the monks bringing mulberry seed, too, we can assume that local black mulberries were to be used.

However, as Susan Whitfield has cautioned,

> like the other stories concerned with the transmission of moriculture and sericulture, the invocation of a Nestorian network simplifies what was probably a long and complex process of transmission across Eurasia over the first few centuries CE, with materials and technologies carried by merchants, monks, diplomats, soldiers and others. This gradually led to the diffusion of both moriculture and sericulture, first in central Asia, then into west Asia and then across the Mediterranean, only reaching Europe rather late.[56]

Also, as we know from Zoe Lady Hart Dyke's account of her trials and tribulations when starting a silk industry in 1950s southern England, it takes a lot more than mulberries and silkworm eggs to get a viable commercial industry off the ground.[57] Suitable temperature-controlled silkworm rooms are needed, as well as a constant supply of mulberry leaves – synchronized in age with the silkworms – and of course the know-how to harvest the cocoons and reel off the silk.

The Arab Silk Trade

The geopolitics of trade in silk took another new turn around 550 CE, when Turkish Bulgar peoples took control of the area from the Black Sea to the borders of China. The Sogdians, an Iranian-speaking people who occupied the fertile valleys of what is now Uzbekistan and Tajikistan, became celebrated traders in Central Asia, acting as go-betweens in trade with China along the overland Silk Routes, especially during the third to eighth centuries CE. Their knowledge of sericulture and the silk trade subsequently became invaluable to the various Turkic kingdoms and empires. With continuing conflicts with the Sassanids and the collapse of the Syrian silk trade following a devastating earthquake (not to mention a plague pandemic), Justinian would have welcomed a new supply of silk brokered by the Sogdians.

By whichever path the silkworms eventually reached the capital of the Byzantine Empire, Constantinople had become a major silk-manufacturing centre by the tenth century CE, with state-controlled workshops producing high-quality silks – rearing silkworms on the native black mulberry.

The real game-changer, of course, came with the Islamic conquests of Central Asia in the seventh and eighth centuries CE. Islamic rule

Gathering mulberry leaves to feed silkworms, 19th century, Chinese painting on rice paper.

Sassanid (Persian) inspired silk cloth from the early Islamic period in Iran.

expanded rapidly throughout the Arabian peninsula in the decade 622–632 CE. Just over a century later, by 750 CE, the Arabs controlled a massive empire, stretching from the Iberian peninsula (southern Spain) and North Africa in the west, via Sicily and Crete to the Chinese border in the east, the Indian border to the south and most of Central Asia to the north. With the former Sassanid Empire now ruled by the Islamic caliphate, there were far-reaching implications in terms of the silk trade.[58]

It would be easy to become sidetracked further with the story of silk, but here our focus has to stay with its rather eclipsed Siamese twin, the mulberry tree.[59] In the next two chapters we will see how both black and white mulberries continued to migrate westwards, but with different timelines and initial driving forces.

three
Lost Angels

Not long before the First World War (in which he was to lose his life), the English poet and writer Edward Thomas was cycling out of London to gather material for his travel diary, *In Pursuit of Spring*. Along the way, his attention was grabbed by some old fruit trees in the gardens of large, old houses. 'The almond, the mulberry, the apple trees in these gardens,' he wrote, 'have a menaced or actually caged loveliness, as of a creature detained from some world far from ours, if they are not, as in some cases they are, the lost angels of ruined paradises' (borrowing a metaphor from Percy Bysshe Shelley's epic poem *Adonais*).[1]

An extraordinary example of one such 'ruined paradise' is an overgrown orchard in the shadow of Syon House in Brentford, just across the River Thames from London's Kew Gardens. Here stand a dozen 'lost angels' – gnarled mulberry trees that some claim are over five hundred years old. Several bear the hallmarks of ancient trees: their heartwood has mostly rotted away, while the outer sapwood has split into what seems like a fairy circle of separate trunks. Some have collapsed onto the ground, sending branches vertically to become future trees in their own right, in a process known as 'layering'.

Other ancient mulberries like these are dotted across England, all of them black mulberries (*Morus nigra*). The story of how they ended up there is one of extraordinary migrations, not always having anything to do with silk.

The Black Mulberry in Antiquity

As we have seen, the origin of the black mulberry is uncertain, but is generally thought to be located within a region roughly corresponding to the Persian Sassanid Empire (224–651 CE), stretching from the Mediterranean in the west to Bactria and Sogdiana in the east (Tajikistan, Uzbekistan and Afghanistan today). References in the Old Testament appear to confirm that the range of the black mulberry included much of the Levant (Egypt and ancient Syria), at least three centuries before the Christian era. However, there is some confusion as to whether the species referred to is actually *M. nigra*.

In the King James English translation of the Old Testament (completed between 1604 and 1611), we read how David defeated the Philistines in the Valley of Rephaim (to the west of Jerusalem):

> And let it be, when thou hearest the sound of going in the tops of the mulberry trees, that then thou shalt bestir thyself: for then shall the LORD go out before thee, to smite the host of the Philistines. (2 Samuel 5:24)

One of several ancient black mulberries at Syon House, near London. The trees may be remnants of the orchard of a 15th-century Brigittine monastery dissolved by Henry VIII between 1536 and 1541. The collapsed branches are layering, producing what looks like a grove of trees, but which all share the same original bole.

The 'mulberry' of the Bible may be a sycamine or sycamore-fig, which is not a *Morus* species but a closely related *Ficus* (fig) species, like this *Ficus sycomorus*, near Abreha and Atsbeha Church in Ethiopia (2012).

The 'going', or 'marching' as it is sometimes translated, is thought to refer to the rustling of leaves. But can we be sure that these were mulberry trees? In the original Hebrew and Aramaic, the trees are called *baca* or *bekha'im*, which modern translations render as 'balsam tree', not 'mulberry'. The trees could, then, have been the Mecca balsam (*Balsamodendron opobalsamum* or *Commiphora gileadensis*) rather than *Morus nigra*.

There was also some confusion in biblical and classical writings between the black mulberry, the *sycomore* and the *sykamine*. As Victor Hehn pointed out in his quirky but seminal *Cultivated Plants and Domestic Animals*, there is little doubt that, when we find the New Comedy poets (*fl.* 350 BCE) writing 'you dye your cheeks with *sycamines* instead of paint,' they were referring to the black mulberry (fruit).[2] And the Greek philosopher Theophrastus, writing about the same time (*fl.* 371–287 BCE), clearly distinguished *sykaminos* (mulberry tree) from *sykaminos Aegyptia* (sycomore).[3]

Some texts that mention the mulberry, especially in the New Testament (originally written in Greek), may have been describing yet another tree altogether. In modern translations of the Bible, we find Jesus saying: 'If you had faith like a grain of mustard seed, you could say to this mulberry tree, "Be uprooted and planted in the sea," and it would obey you' (Luke 17:6).

But in the King James translation He says: 'If ye had faith as a grain of mustard seed, ye might say unto this sycamine tree, "Be thou plucked up by the root, and be thou planted in the sea," and it should obey you.'

References to mulberry, *sycamore* and *sykamine* in the Bible could all be pointing to the sycamore-fig or fig-mulberry (*Ficus sycomorus*). This is an impressive tree found growing wild in Egypt and Lebanon, which later became naturalized in Palestine and Israel. Indeed, the New Study Bible (Luke 19:4) uses the term 'sycamore-fig', which is described in a note as 'a sturdy tree 30 to 40 feet [9–12 m] high, with a short trunk, and spreading branches, capable of holding a grown man'. This could also describe a black mulberry.

Like the mulberry, the sycamore-fig is a member of the *Moraceae* family, with leaves that resemble those of M. *nigra*, hence the possible confusion at a time when taxonomy was based on superficial characteristics and resemblances. The jury is therefore out on whether the black mulberry is indigenous to the Holy Land or was introduced later.

Romans and Mulberries

By the time of the Roman philosopher and physician Galen (130–210 CE), the mulberry confusion seems to have gone away. According to Victor Hehn, the Greek root μωρός (*moros*) had by then been adopted for the mulberry, Latinized to *morus*. When Virgil refers to *sanguinea morus* (the blood-coloured mulberry), he obviously means the black mulberry.

Just to complicate matters further, though, the superficial similarity of the blackberry's and the mulberry's fruit meant that they were not always distinguished. For clarity, the Romans came to specify *morum celsae arboris* (the mulberry of the tall tree) when they meant black mulberry fruit, and *morus celsae* for the tree itself – hence the modern Italian *gelso* for both mulberry fruit and tree. A similar confusion between the blackberry and mulberry can be found in medieval English writings several centuries later. Archbishop Aelfric, in his *Vocabulary* (late tenth century), gives a key to identifying these plants by the colour of their ripe and unripe fruit – '*morus vel rubus, mor-beam*' (black or red, mulberry) and '*flavi vel mori, blace-berian*' (yellow or black, blackberry).[4]

The Roman lyric poet Horace, writing in Italy at the end of the first century BCE, was unambiguously referring to the black mulberry – as a fruit – when he said: 'I'll give him health, who when his meals are done, eats juicy mulberries, pluck'd before the sun doth rise too high, and scorch with heat of noon.'[5]

While there is mixed evidence for the presence of the black mulberry in the Holy Land in antiquity, then, it was well established in Italy at least by the time of the Roman Empire. The tree is clearly shown in a mosaic uncovered in the House of Venus Marina in Pompeii, which was engulfed by lava and ash when Vesuvius erupted in August 79 CE.[6] Mulberry trees are also depicted in the peristyle of the House of the Bull and a mosaic in the House of the Faun.[7]

Interestingly, a plant survey carried out by a German botanist, Joakim Frederik Schouw, during archaeological excavations at Pompeii in 1854, found no evidence of the white mulberry in the area around Pompeii at the time Vesuvius erupted, even though it is present today.[8] It was to be another 1,400 years before this species arrived in Italy.

The Romans took black mulberries with them when they occupied new territories. They seem to have been grown by the elite for their fruit, rather than to keep the troops healthy. After the Roman armies annexed Provence around 121 BCE, Julius Caesar led a successful campaign to conquer Gaul in 58 BCE. They settled and stayed for the next five hundred years, leaving an indelible impression on the urban and rural landscapes of France. Remains of black mulberries have been found in a Roman well as far north as the Armorican Massif (modern-day Brittany). Evidence of Roman black mulberries has also been found in sites across Europe, from Aachen, Cologne and Trier to northern Germany.[9]

Long after the Romans left Gaul in 486 CE, black mulberries continued to be grown for their medicinal value and highly nutritious fruit. There are records from the eleventh century CE of a black mulberry tree in the medieval monastery of Saint-Guénolé in Landévennec, near Brest in Brittany. Charlemagne (742–814 CE) included black mulberries in his Capitulary of 802 CE, listing desirable plants to be grown on the royal estates.[10] Mulberries were, he stipulated, to be used for making wine – a sensible use for the abundant fruit, which perishes almost

Mulberry fruit were included in some mosaics buried by the eruption of Vesuvius, such as this one at the House of the Faun in Pompeii.

Lost Angels

Mineralized black mulberry seed from an early Roman site (Insula IX) at Silchester, UK. 50–60–70 CE.

as soon as it is plucked. Charlemagne's ordinance even stipulated that stewards handling the fruit (and other foods) should maintain scrupulous hygiene, washing their hands regularly.

The Romans also introduced black mulberries to Britain when they established the city of Londinium around 43 CE. Archaeologists found black mulberry seeds when excavating waterlogged Roman sites by the Thames in the 1970s, near to what became the old Billingsgate Fish Market.[11] The fruit of the black mulberry does not travel (as mentioned, it's quick to turn to mush and, unlike the white mulberry, cannot be dried), so the seeds must either have been brought over to be planted, or else have come from fruit harvested from trees that the Romans had planted nearby. British palaeobotanist Clement Reid also found black mulberry seeds during excavations of the Roman city of Silchester, in Hampshire, in 1901–2.[12] (It should be remembered that the climate in Britain was more temperate 2,000 years ago; the Romans also grew grapes, medlars and figs.[13])

Moors and Mulberries

If the Romans had been the main vector for the spread of black mulberries to France and Britain in the first centuries CE, it was the Arabs (Moors) who introduced the tree to Spain and North Africa – this time not so much as a source of food and medicine for humans, as a food for silkworms.

In 751 CE, after defeating the Chinese Tang army in the Talas Valley, between modern-day Kyrgyzstan and Kazakhstan, the Islamic army are believed to have captured skilled silk weavers among their prisoners of war. According to the Chinese historian Xinru Liu, soon after this victory, mulberry trees started to be exported for the first time as a commercial crop, 'all the way to North Africa and Southern Spain'.[14] This is probably a simplification of a complex and more long-term diffusion of the mulberry westwards and southwards, though. By this time black – and even white – mulberries were being grown for silk outside China and the caliphate would have learned of this as they expanded east.[15]

Although white mulberries may have been growing in Central Asia by the early Middle Ages, it is likely that the first wave of Moorish sericulture in Spain, Portugal and North Africa was centred on the black mulberry, *M. nigra*, which was already abundant around the eastern Mediterranean. The Moors would therefore have introduced the black mulberry to these countries at the same time as the silkworm.[16]

Spain continued to be an important European producer of silk, with exports reaching a peak in the fourteenth and fifteenth centuries, particularly following the establishment of the port of Almeria. Archives from the 1520s show that mulberries were particularly abundant in the region around the port: '[The region] had suffered little from the transition from Islam to Christianity; the ex-Moorish population . . . lived in small, intensively cultivated, terraced oases among the steppe and badlands. The principal crops recorded were olives and mulberries.'[17]

At one time in Spain, a person's wealth – and the tax they owed – was calculated on the basis of the number of mulberry trees they possessed or the quantity of cocoons of silk they harvested.[18] By the fourteenth century, unlike in the Byzantine Empire, which concentrated silk production in state workshops, Spanish raw silk was increasingly produced by a distributed network of cottage industries, each with a few mulberries and rooms reserved for raising silkworms.

Terraces of mulberry trees changed the landscape of Spain, with medieval and early-modern terraces becoming 'the most conspicuous features of Mediterranean cultural landscapes'.[19] A lease dated 1528 for a vineyard in Tarval, near Almeria, in southeastern Spain includes: 'three terraces which contain eight *tahullas* of land, and it has thirteen fig-trees and five mulberries'.[20]

The Spanish silk industry nevertheless went into decline just as French sericulture was on the rise, in the sixteenth century CE. However, the colonizing Spanish conquistadores did start a successful silk industry in New Spain (Mexico) in the early years of the sixteenth century. Finding a variety of red mulberry (*Morus rubra*) already growing there, they brought *Bombyx mori* eggs to the region around Oaxaca in 1531 CE. The project got off to a very good start but, barely sixty years later, the young colonial industry was already on the wane, partly as the indigenous labour force was decimated by new diseases introduced from Spain, but also due to fierce competition from imported silks arriving on galleons from Manila in the Philippines.[21]

Refugees, Exiles and Mulberries

The Mediterranean island of Sicily played a critical role in the migrations of the black mulberry westwards and the spread of sericulture to the rest of Italy, North Africa and finally into France. Sicily came under Norman rule in 1091 CE, having been recaptured from the Arabs by the Byzantines. It became a melting pot of languages, religions and cultures – Greek, Arab, Roman and Norman – and

El Masnou (Spain). White mulberries are common street trees in parts of Spain.

was noted for its tolerance. It came into its own in the early twelfth century, under King Roger II, when the kingdom of Sicily included most of Italy south of Rome.

Sicily's geographic situation at the centre of the Mediterranean made it a perfect location for trade with Europe, North Africa and the Middle East. Roger II even invited experienced Arab and Greek administrators to help him run his kingdom. He built up a powerful fleet, led by a series of admirals or *emirs*, the most powerful being George of Antioch, born in Syria but with Greek ancestry, who had been living in Tunisia.

But it wasn't all harmony and peace. In 1147 CE, George launched a series of attacks on Greece, notably the Peloponnese peninsula and the city of Thebes. Having started in the sixth century CE, the culture of black mulberry trees for sericulture had become so important here that the peninsula came to be known as Morea, after the Greek word for mulberry – possibly also because it is shaped rather like a mulberry leaf.

In Thebes, George pillaged the celebrated Byzantine silk manufactures, which had become the largest producers of silks in the Empire, relegating even Constantinople to second place.[22] He also captured some of the city's Jewish silk weavers – who had been banned from operating in Constantinople under the strict Imperial monopoly on silk – taking them with him to Palermo. Here, they were put to work to help establish a Sicilian silk-weaving industry, which became the most important in the West for a while. The extensive royal parks of the Norman and Swabian kings of Sicily later probably contained plantations of black (and subsequently white) mulberry trees.

Several times in the course of history the forced migration of silk weavers, along with their knowledge of sericulture, has become a vector for the migration of the industry, together with its mulberries and silkworms. After the sack of Constantinople in 1204 CE during the Fourth Crusade, many skilled silk workers fled the city and settled in Italy – notably in Lucca, but also in Florence, Genoa, Milan and Venice.[23]

Later, the Alhambra decree of 1492 CE forced Jews who would not convert to Catholicism to leave Spain. Hundreds of thousands settled in the Ottoman Empire, notably Tiberias in southern Syria, on the shores of the Sea of Galilee (now part of Israel). It was here in 1561 that a Portuguese diplomat, Joseph Nasi, started a silk industry, with backing from the sultan, and planted mulberry trees on a large scale – including, by then, white mulberries. A century later, in 1685, the Edict of Fontainebleau (also known as the Revocation of the Edict of Nantes) promulgated by Louis XIV of France ended the freedom of Protestant Huguenots to practise their religion, causing a mass exodus of religious refugees to northern Europe. Among them were many skilled silk weavers – but we are jumping ahead of our story.

Black Mulberry Sericulture in France

French sericulture based on the white mulberry only started in earnest from the early sixteenth century. Sericulture based on the black mulberry, however, had begun two hundred years earlier in an area known as the Comtat Venaissin, with encouragement from the Catholic Church. The Comtat roughly corresponds to the Vaucluse region today and includes the picturesque Lubéron massif. With its administrative centre in Avignon, the region was bequeathed to the Holy See in 1271 CE. After a year of bitter disputes between the cardinals of France and Italy following the death of Pope Benedict XI, they finally elected a Frenchman, Raymond Bertrand de Got, as Pope Clement V, in 1305 CE.

Under pressure from the French king, Philip IV, Clement refused to move to Rome and, instead, established a papal enclave in Avignon. This remained the centre of the papacy until 1376 CE, when Pope Gregory XI returned the see to Rome. The relative tolerance of the Catholics attracted persecuted Jews to Avignon and the Comtat from Italy and elsewhere in France, including weavers and those familiar with the craft of silk-making. It was also a period of economic demise for Italy, so we can see how silk weaving and sericulture could become established in the Comtat around this time. The first indigenous French silk was produced on Avignon looms – a mix of wool and silk called *doucette*, and, later, damask (after the city of Damascus), a satin fabric first developed in Syria.[24]

There is a hypothesis that black mulberry trees were also imported via the Pyrenees from Spain and planted in the Cévennes during the thirteenth century. Archives in Languedoc record a certain Raymond de Gaussorgues of Anduze as being officially registered as a *trahanderius* or 'silk reeler' as early as 1296 CE. And there are records of silkworm eggs being sold to peasant farmers in the towns of Mialet and Saint-Jean-du-Gard in the early fourteenth century, with the resulting cocoons of silk being reeled locally and then traded in Paris.[25]

It was not until the fifteenth century that French sericulture began to get official recognition, first around Lyons on the Rhône river, then at Tours on the Loire. In letters patent, dated 24 November 1466 CE, Louis XI (1423–1483) sought to encourage this nascent industry in Lyons, having seen how prosperous Italy and Spain had become through silk manufacture and weaving. Louis XI exempted French silk weavers from paying taxes, and brought silkworm eggs, silk weavers and spinners over from Italy, presumably using the leaves of any black mulberries that had become established by then.

But the weavers and peasant farmers of Lyons were reluctant to turn their hand to the unfamiliar practice of sericulture, which involved cultivating mulberry trees, raising silkworms and reeling thread from cocoons, rather than concentrating on what they already did so well – simply weaving imported silk thread. So, Louis XI moved the enterprise to his favourite castle at Plessis-lez-Tours in the Loire Valley. According to an eighteenth-century account by Jean-Marie Roland de la Platrière (an inspector of silk manufactures in Lyons), Louis XI appointed an Italian, François le Calabrois (Francesco della Calabria), to plant mulberries on his estate at Tours.

Thirty years later, they had grown into 'fine trees, 15 to 18 inches [38–46 cm] in diameter'.[26]

Louis XI died in 1483, before he could see his project blossom, so it fell to his then thirteen-year-old son, Charles VIII (1470–1898), to give sericulture the boost his father had dreamed of. This time it would be based on the white mulberry, first introduced to Italy a few decades earlier, but already being widely adopted, as we shall see in the next chapter.

Black Mulberries Cross the Channel (Again)

The spectacular rise in silk weaving in France from the fourteenth century was centred predominantly on Lyons and Tours and at first mostly used imported raw silk thread. Over the next five centuries successive rulers tried to get French sericulture off the ground, to stem the haemorrhage of money seeping into Italy, Spain and the Middle East to buy raw silk. This translated into spasmodic mass plantings of the unfamiliar white mulberry species, which sometimes met with opposition. Meanwhile, the (by then) more familiar black mulberry continued to be used for French sericulture, especially in the Cévennes and Languedoc regions.

At the turn of the seventeenth century the celebrated horticulturalist Olivier de Serres was overseeing a massive expansion of sericulture under Henri IV based on the white mulberry, as we shall see in the next chapter. Around the same time, the English and Scottish thrones became united with the accession of James I of England and VI of Scotland in 1603. James had been watching Henri IV's efforts with great interest. Mulberries were once again about to cross the Channel – this time en masse.

After the Romans left England around 410 CE, mulberries probably continued to be grown as fruit trees on the site of their former settlements. Some undoubtedly layered as successive 'phoenix' scions, regenerating from the ancient stumps of senescent original Roman trees.[27] They were also grown in medieval monasteries

The black mulberry is often associated with monasteries. This one stands in the ruins of Lesnes Abbey near London, destroyed by Henry VIII during the Dissolution.

– possibly encouraged by monks returning from Rome who had tasted the fruit there.

When Henry VIII and his first minister, Thomas Cromwell, dissolved the Catholic monasteries between 1536 and 1541, some were spared destruction and eventually passed into the hands of those in favour with the king. The new owners turned the monasteries into palatial country houses, complete with any mulberry trees they may have had. Fresh mulberries were a favourite at Tudor banquets and offered an opportunity for one-upmanship: if you wanted fresh mulberries you had to grow them in your own kitchen garden. There was, then, a vested interest in keeping any mature mulberry trees in the orchards of the former monasteries – hence the 'lost angels' at Syon House, which had been a Brigittine monastery in the fifteenth century, with an orchard exactly where the mulberry grove is today.

James I's interest in mulberries, though, was not for their fruit but their leaves – to feed the silkworms he planned to raise on English trees. It was obvious that the few medieval black mulberry trees dotted around England in country houses and former monasteries would not be enough to sustain a silk industry to rival those on the continent. He sought the best advice on how to go about starting a silk industry and called on a Plymouth-born merchant and customs official, William Stallenge, to commission and publish a translation of writings on mulberries and silkworms by leading French expert Olivier de Serres, adviser to and friend of Henri IV of France. Stallenge had previously been employed by the extremely powerful William Cecil (Lord Burghley) under Elizabeth I, so was already in favour with the court. In Tudor times (not unlike today) it was not so much what you knew, but who you knew . . .

In 1607 the 62-year-old Stallenge oversaw the publication of *The Perfect Use of Silk-wormes, and their Benefit*, 'done out of the French originall' by Nicholas Geffe. Tributes in the book to Geffe's industry in bringing this translation to the British public heaped praise on him and the likely fortunes that home-grown mulberries would bring to the nation, not least by saving money on imported silk:

> The tree acquainting with the British soyle
> And the true use unto our people taught
> Shall trebble ten times recompense the toile
> (From forraine parts) of him it hither brought.[28]

The circles of influence and favour were indeed small at the time – Nicholas Geffe had ties with Francis Bacon, who became attorney general under James I.[29] Bacon was the cousin of Robert Cecil (son of Lord Burghley). But this may not have been useful – there was no love lost between the rival cousins and Cecil seemed at best not to want to help Bacon's advance and, at worst, actively hoped to hinder it.

To start his home-grown silk project, James wrote letters to the 'Lords Lieutenants of the Severall Shires of England' and their deputies, asking them 'to persuade and require such as are of ability to buy and distribute in your county the number of ten thousand mulberry plants, which shall be distributed to them at the rate of three farthings a plant, or at six shillings the hundred containing five score plants'. More affordable packets of mulberry seeds were to be provided for the less well-off to plant the following spring, so that they could establish plantations to feed thousands of silkworms. James also promised to print 'a plain instruction and direction, both for the increasing the said mulberry trees, the breeding of the silkworms, and all other things needful to be understood for work every way so commendable and profitable'. This took the form of a pamphlet published by Stallenge in 1609.[30] This was, in fact, a translation of an earlier French pamphlet by Jean-Baptiste Letellier, which had been published in 1603.[31] A copy of the king's letter was included as an annex to Stallenge's version.

Setting the example (as Henri IV had done with Serres in the Tuileries gardens in Paris), James paid Stallenge 'the sum of £935 for the charge of 4 acres [1.6 ha] of land taken in for His Majesty's use, near to his Palace of Westminster, for the planting of Mulberry trees, together with the charge of walling, levelling and planting thereof for Mulberry trees'.[32] This became the celebrated (and later notorious) Mulberry Garden in the grounds of St James's Palace – on a site that corresponds to the northwest corner of the garden behind today's Buckingham Palace and part of the adjacent Green Park. The land had been 'purchased' (requisitioned) from the Abbots of Westminster.

James's consort, Anne of Denmark, shared his enthusiasm and established another mulberry plantation, complete with silkworm nursery, at Greenwich Palace. Although a veteran black mulberry survives today in a walled garden, in what is now the Queen's Orchard at the northwest corner of Greenwich Park, there is no reliably established trace of this plantation, or exactly where it was. It may even have been in the grounds of Charlton House, a couple of

Detail of a portrait of an 'Unknown Lady' wearing a silk dress embroidered with silkworms and mulberry leaves. The sitter, once thought to be Elizabeth I, is possibly Anne of Denmark, consort to James I, who was passionate about the king's sericulture project. The painting is in Parham House, West Sussex, UK.

kilometres east, which was completed in 1611 as residence for the tutor to Prince Henry, James's eldest son (who was to die of typhoid fever a year later). An old black mulberry survives at Charlton, too, although its location does not obviously point to its having been part of a plantation.

Anne established another mulberry grove at the Royal Palace at Oatlands, Elmbridge, in Surrey. At Oatlands she commissioned Inigo Jones to build an elegant two-storey silkworm house, which can be seen in the background of a 1617 portrait of her painted by Paul van Somers (1574–1619).[33] John Bonoeil, whom James later entrusted with overseeing a sericulture project across the Atlantic in Virginia, was appointed Keeper of the Royal Gardens, Vines and Silkworms at Oatlands. In the first years of the silk project James put considerable energy into trying to get it off the ground. William Stallenge and François de Verton (also known as Seigneur de la Forêt) were given sole rights to distribute mulberry trees and silkworms throughout the counties, along with instructions on how to rear them, following up the terms of James's decree. Stallenge and Verton had 10,000 saplings sent from Languedoc in the south of France to offer to each of a list of thirteen counties.

In her detailed account of James's silk project the late Joan Thirsk, the prominent economic and social historian, found that not all of the earls, dukes and lords bought into James's project, causing Stallenge and Verton to leave empty-handed. Some did, however: in Northampton, two deputy lieutenants took a large number; the Earl of Leicester took 3,000; and Sir Henry Pierrepont took 1,000 in Nottingham. Several others took 'a good number', while some, like the Duke of Rutland, refused to have anything to do with the scheme whatsoever.[34]

We know that some colleges at Cambridge University also bought into James's scheme. A few wonderful old trees have survived to this day at Christ's, Corpus Christi, Jesus and Emmanuel Colleges in Cambridge. College records show bills for the purchase of black mulberries, for preparing land for them, and also the construction of 'sheds' to house the silkworms.[35] There is also a veteran black mulberry in Pembroke College, Oxford, and another at Balliol.

While Verton and Stallenge were doing the rounds of the counties, James I paid £50 to a certain Munton (or Mountain) Jennings to plant mulberries and make 'a place for silkworms' at his favourite palace at Theobalds (Hertfordshire), which he had exchanged for his palace at Hatfield with Robert Cecil, First Earl of Salisbury. In 1611 Cecil sent his newly appointed head gardener, John Tradescant the Elder, to the Low Countries and Paris to buy mulberries for the grounds of Hatfield House, which he rebuilt in the Jacobean style. According to Linda Levy Peck, Cecil was keen to hedge his bets over where the profit was to be made on silk – would it be on imports, for which he had been granted a share of duties by the king, or on home-grown silk?[36]

Records held in the Hatfield House archives show Tradescant's bills for black mulberries, purchased in Leiden, Rouen and Paris. According to Sarah Whale, archivist to the Salisbury Estate,

> At Leiden in Holland Tradescant bought various flowers and fruit trees, including two mulberry trees costing six shillings (Bills 58/3). The bill is dated 5 January 1612. At Rouen Tradescant bought seventeen 'blak mulberry trees at 2s the peece' and also spent £10 on 104 trees: 'peaches mulberyes and cheryes called Biggerawes' (Bills 58/31). This bill is also dated 5 January 1612.[37]

Other accounts suggest that in all Tradescant planted five hundred mulberries at Hatfield, although there is no trace of these trees today.[38] However, one of four ornamental black mulberries – possibly even planted before Tradescant's time – is still growing in the formal West Garden at Hatfield, adjacent to the old Tudor Palace.

Whether planted for silk or not, mulberries must have been the talk of the town in the early seventeenth century, especially in circles close to the king and Robert Cecil. This could explain the presence of another 'lost angel' – a veteran black mulberry in a walled courtyard behind the Tudor Canonbury Tower in north London, where Cecil's cousin, Francis Bacon, lived for several years from 1617. Tradescant had moved on from Hatfield to a post as head gardener to Lord Wotton, in Canterbury, a year earlier, but Bacon's essay on the design of the ideal formal garden – written in 1608 but not published until 1625 – may have influenced the layout of the East Garden at Hatfield.[39] Those close circles of influence again...

The Wrong Mulberries?

James's sericulture project did not produce the promised results in England, with Stallenge's choice of *Morus nigra* often blamed for the failure. Successful Italian, French and Spanish sericulture had long converted to the white mulberry, *Morus alba*, so highly prized by the Chinese. In his 'bible' on mulberries and silk (by that time available in English, thanks to the efforts of Nicholas Geffe), Olivier de Serres clearly explains that, when starting a sericulture venture from scratch, the white mulberry is always to be preferred over the black for feeding silkworms. But he does not rule out the usefulness of the black mulberry:

> If your land be already planted with blacke Mulberries, keep you there without affecting your selfe to accompany them with white, for the reason alleaged: but being a question to begin the husbandrie, having not any Mulberries, of one sort, nor other, preferring the better before the good; you shall always chuse the white for your Mulberrie-yard... The white Mulberries do more easily take, and grow than the black, advancing more in two yeeres, than the other in sixe.[40]

Serres also emphasized that black mulberries were being used successfully for sericulture in some parts of Europe, notably 'Lombardie, and hitherwards in *Anduze*, and *Alez*, and in other places towards the

Sevenes of *Languedoc*, where great profit is made of the silke which comes of the blacke Mulberries'. His main criticism of black mulberry leaves was that the silk tends to be 'grosse, strong and heavie' and therefore not able to be used for the finest and lightest silks, which of course would fetch higher prices. He also cautioned not to mix the two 'meates', but to stick with whichever species was widely available locally. Sericulture in the Cévennes did, though, convert to the white mulberry on a large scale by the nineteenth century.

Black mulberries were already growing in England, and several must already have been of considerable age – testimony to their ability to withstand the British climate. The white mulberry, on the other hand, was an unknown quantity; it had never been grown successfully in England and was more likely to be associated with the warm, continental climate of southern France, Italy and Spain. This may have encouraged Stallenge in his choice of *M. nigra* over *M. alba* to plant in England.

According to the Scottish botanist and garden designer John Claudius Loudon, writing in the early nineteenth century, the failure of sericulture to take off in the seventeenth century wasn't even a matter of species, but simply one of climate. 'In warm climates, such as Persia,' he says, 'the leaves of *M. nigra* are sufficiently succulent for feeding the silkworm; but in colder countries they do not answer equally well.'[41] Serres had also warned that silkworms would not thrive in damp places:

> our Wormes are never well disposed, fed with leaves growing in a waterish place . . . The raines happening on the course of this food, strangely hinder the Wormes, as if they chance towards the end of their life, than when they are in the great force of devouring: for that the wette leaves do breed them dangerous diseases.[42]

Britain was passing through the Little Ice Age at the time, with long and bitterly cold winters. The Thames froze over ten times in

Veteran black mulberry on the site of Sayes Court, the house of diarist John Evelyn.

the seventeenth century, and frost fairs on the river were not unusual.[43] It had even frozen over in the winter of 1608, just as James was drafting letters to his lord lieutenants asking them to back his sericulture project. It is probably not the mulberries that suffered the ill effects of Britain's protracted cold, though – and there are dozens of seventeenth-century mulberries still alive today as proof. After all, Pliny had called *Morus nigra* 'the wisest of trees', for not venturing to put out its leaves until the frosts were gone. The problem for James's venture may have been the difficulty in timing the hatching of silkworm eggs with the appearance of the first mulberry leaves. A heavy and long winter would mean a late spring, possibly threatening the whole year's harvest of silkworm cocoons.

Efforts to grow (black) mulberries for silk in England continued spasmodically under the Stuarts in the seventeenth century and into the early eighteenth century. In 1630, when John Bonoeil died, James I's heir, Charles I, appointed John Tradescant the Elder (and his 22-year-old son, John Tradescant the Younger) to take over the gardens at Oatlands and paid him a further £100 a year (equivalent to about £12,000 today – or four times the wages of a skilled tradesman) to look after the Mulberry Garden in London. Like Anne of Denmark, Charles's queen, Henrietta Maria, also enjoyed spending time at Oatlands. She was, after all, the daughter of none other than Henri IV of France and Marie de Médicis – who had championed mulberries and sericulture in France on a large scale. Born at the Louvre Palace in 1609 she must have been familiar with her father's mulberries in the Tuileries, even if she was only a year old when he was assassinated.

After Charles I was beheaded and Oliver Cromwell's parliamentary interlude had passed, Charles II tried to promote sericulture in England when he was restored to the throne in 1660. By this time the Mulberry Garden in St James's Park was no longer used for rearing silkworms but was now a pleasure garden, popular with certain strata of London society and not always the most wholesome. Oliver Cromwell had closed the more upmarket Spring Garden (in Vauxhall), which had been a popular outdoor venue for high society. According to the seventeenth century diarist John Evelyn, in a barbed entry on 10 May 1654 during Cromwell's interregnum, 'My Lady Gerrard treated us at the Mulberry garden, now ye onely place of refreshment about the towne for persons of ye best quality to be exceedingly cheated at.'[44]

Fourteen years later, when Charles II had returned from exile in France, Evelyn's contemporary, Samuel Pepys, wrote of going to the Mulberry Garden on several occasions and enjoying the food. But he did not have a high opinion of the garden either – or the people it attracted. The first time he went there, on 20 May 1668, he found it 'a very silly place, worse than Spring-garden, and but little company, and those a rascally, whoring, roguing sort of people, only a wilderness here, that is somewhat pretty, but rude'.[45] But this was nothing new; writing in 1649, the politician and lawyer Clement Walker had already referred to 'new-erected sodoms and spintries [brothels and places of debauchery] at the Mulberry Garden at S. James's'.[46]

Sericulture was still a subject of academic interest in England in the late seventeenth century, if not a profitable industry. On 18 February 1669, John Evelyn writes of the presentation to the Royal Society (which he had helped to establish) of an 'incomparable History of the Silkworm' by an Italian anatomist and physician, 'Signor [*sic*] Malpighi'.[47] However, in his *Systema Agriculturae* of 1687, John Worlidge concluded that sericulture was doomed in England because no one was willing to plant enough mulberry trees to meet the demand that industrial-scale silk production would require. It would remain a hobby for aristocrats, he wrote, who might make enough silk for a few pairs of stockings and gloves.[48]

With the influx of Huguenot weavers after the Revocation of the Edict of Nantes in 1685, there was to be a last-ditch attempt at sericulture in England. In 1720 the Raw Silk Company planted 2,000 mulberry trees, both black and white, on a large plot of land in Chelsea that had once belonged to Sir Thomas More, Henry VIII's ill-fated lord chancellor. The project attracted investors via an early

Black mulberry on the site of the Raw Silk Company's plantation in Chelsea, London, c. 1720. Now in a private garden.

form of stock exchange, but by 1723 the company was bankrupt. The land, silkworm house and trees were sold off. Most were grubbed out and the land developed over the next two hundred years for housing. But at least one old black mulberry survives from this period, in the middle of a lawn behind residential apartments on Elm Park Road, visible from the Fulham Road.

The arrival of the white mulberry in Europe in the early fifteenth century eventually brought the large-scale migrations of the black mulberry to an end. Now it would once again only be planted for its fruit, shade and natural elegance as a landscape tree. As Victor Hehn put it:

The Persian provinces on the Caspian Sea and Italy and France in Europe, those silk-countries of the West, are now, in the districts where the industry flourishes, covered all over with cut and despoiled white mulberry-trees; it is only here and there in remote, lag-behind districts that the mulberry-tree of the ancients is still found nourishing a spinning-worm that produces a coarser kind of silk.[49]

four
Mulberry Mania

❦

The cultivation of mulberry trees has always been an integral part of the systematic production and reeling of silk cocoons (sericulture), which started in China around 4,700 years ago. Wherever sericulture (rather than weaving silk thread into textiles) has been practised, during its long, slow journey from ancient China and northern India to just about every continent in the world, the State – in whatever form it took – has invariably played a key role. This has not usually been as entrepreneur, but as facilitator, regulator or autocratic legislator. The State frequently derived taxes from the sale of silk and also on holdings of mulberry trees. It sometimes offered rewards for planting trees – and fines for not doing so.

Detailed descriptions of Chinese mulberry cultivation techniques were written down during the Western Han dynasty (206 BCE–9 CE) in the *Fan Shengzhi shu* (The Book of Fan Shengzhi).[1] These include planting mulberry seed along with millet and suggest that a form of coppicing was being used: 'When the mulberry plants are as high as the millet, cut them down with a sickle close to the ground. Next spring mulberry suckers will spring out. Such mulberry trees are convenient for plucking and management because of their shortness.'[2] According to a chapter on mulberry cultivation in a much later text, *Qimin Yaoshu* (533–44 CE; Essential Techniques for the Common People), similar techniques were still in use, with mulberry seedlings first being grown in nurseries then inter-planted with other crops, like beans.

Mulberry dyke fish-pond system in China.

In another early farming technique (sometimes known as the 'well-field' system), a large area of land was divided into nine equal squares, with the landowner living in the central square and serfs independently cultivating (and living off) the land in the eight surrounding squares. The central square was farmed communally by all the serfs. Only produce from this square would be offered to aristocrats and rulers, as a form of taxation. In this system, the serf family was the production unit, as part of a 'man-farming, woman-weaving' rural economy dating to before 800 BCE. Commonly grown crops included mulberries for sericulture.[3]

Another ancient technique, which is still in use in rural areas of China today, is the 'mulberry dyke and fish-pond system', notably found in the Pearl River delta of Guangdong (the mainland adjacent to Hong Kong). In this system mulberry trees are planted on dykes enclosing a fish pond. The faeces of the silkworms and any mulberry leaf waste are used to feed fish in the pond. The pond silt is, in turn, used to fertilize the mulberry trees. This is an ancient example of what is known today as 'integrated farm management' and is still practised on a large scale around Huzhou on Lake Taihu in the Yangtze River delta, about 80 kilometres (50 mi.) inland from Shanghai.[4]

During the first millennium BCE the Chinese gradually moved southwards, while devastating flooding of the Yellow River repeatedly wiped out farmlands and whole villages. Vast deposits of silt from the Loess Plateau even shifted the course of the river (26 times over the past 3,000 years).[5] By the Eastern Han dynasty (25 BCE–220 CE) China's sericulture had already shifted towards the plains of the Yangtze River basin, cultivating indigenous species of white mulberry (especially *M. alba* and *M. bombycis*). The warmer climate of southern China was also more favourable for sericulture, even allowing more than one harvest of mulberry leaves in a year.

State incentives alternated with more coercive tactics. During the Northern Wei dynasty (386–534 CE), for example, when northern China was ruled by Tuoba Turks from the steppe, farmers there were required to plant fifty mulberry trees for every 2 hectares (5 ac) of farmland provided by the government.[6] During the Tang dynasty this was reduced to just two mulberries for each farm. In the Sung dynasty (960–1127 CE) the number of mulberries a civil servant had

Mulberry plantation on banks of the Grand Canal, Huzhou, China, c. 1853–6, in Robert Fortune, *A Residence Among the Chinese* (1857).

planted became one of the criteria used to decide if he would be promoted. A civil service job was highly coveted, but very hard to get. These punitive tactics changed in the Mongol Yuan dynasty (1271–1368 CE), when farmers were given help and advice on sericulture and the cultivation of mulberries.

By the Ming dynasty (1368–1644 CE) the old punitive approach returned, with farmers being required to plant six hundred trees in three years. Nevertheless, during this period and the Qing dynasty (1644–1911 CE), the cultivation of mulberries for sericulture brought about an unprecedented prosperity. The Scottish botanist and plant collector Robert Fortune, travelling through the region around Huzhou (romanized as Hoo-chow) in the 1850s, records seeing extensive mulberry plantations.[7] According to illustrations accompanying Fortune's account of his journey, these mulberry fields were often located beside canals and lakes and included both full-height trees and coppiced bushes, which are easier to harvest. The *Fan Shengzhi Shu* text from the Western Han period already refers to the advantages of keeping mulberry trees as low bushes, around 2,000 years ago.

Europe's First White Mulberry?

There is very little conclusive documentary information about how and when white mulberry cultivation for silk was introduced to the Middle East and eastern Mediterranean. In his celebrated *Travels*, Marco Polo makes no mention of mulberry trees on his outward journey to Khanbaliq (modern-day Beijing) via the Middle East and Central Asia. Setting off from Venice in 1271 as a seventeen-year-old with his father and uncle, he only returned 24 years later in 1295. Marco records seeing silk weaving (in Baghdad and Persia) but does not report mulberry trees, even though they must certainly have been there – whether white or black. It is not until his later journey eastwards again from Khanbaliq, on a mission on behalf of the great Mongol emperor Kublai Khan, that we first read of mulberries and silk in any detail.

In Taiyuanfu city (Shanxi province), he writes that 'there is . . . no end of silk, for they have a profusion of mulberry trees and silkworms'.[8] And the area around Hezhongfu (modern-day Puzhou), with its mountains and fertile plains, was 'full of mulberry trees'.[9] These would have been the indigenous *M. alba*, but Polo would not have known the difference from mulberries he may have seen in Italy – he was after all just a young merchant and not a botanist in search of exotic plants. Polo's *Travels* were written down and embroidered by the author Rusticello da Pisa, with whom he shared a prison cell back in Italy, but his descriptions of seeing mulberry trees do not seem to be candidates for embellishment.

As we have seen, sericulture was first introduced to countries around the eastern Mediterranean from Central Asia and would initially have been based on the native black mulberry. The substitution of *M. alba* for *M. nigra* was likely a slow process at first, possibly with white-mulberry moriculture becoming established towards the eastern limit of the natural range of *M. nigra*: in the Fergana Valley and around major trading hubs on the Silk Road, such as Samarkand in modern-day Uzbekistan – a country that claims to have a history of traditional sericulture going back 2,000 years or more.[10]

The first documented attempt to grow *M. alba* in Europe was in Pescia, Italy, about 15 kilometres (9 mi.) east of Lucca in Tuscany, when Francesco Buonvicino brought back some plants from his travels in the Orient in 1434.[11] Buonvicino's white mulberry arrived some two hundred years after Sicily had begun producing its own silk thread using black mulberry leaves. The spread of sericulture in Italy in the thirteenth century responded to a vacuum in the supply of silk from the usual Byzantine and Chinese sources, just at a time when Europeans were increasingly eager to lay their hands on the wonderfully iridescent material that Crusaders had brought with them on their return from the Holy Land and Constantinople.

The timing was perfect. As historian Rebecca Woodward Wendelken put it, 'More local weaving of silk in Spain, the decline of the Byzantine sources and quality, and the turmoil of the Crusades in

Francesco Buonvicini with the first mulberry sapling, Pescia, Italy.

the Middle East, combined with a decrease in Chinese trade due to the Mongol invasions left European silk weavers in short supply of imported raw materials.'[12] The thirteenth-century Mongol invasions created havoc for sericulture in Central Asia and around the Black Sea, by destroying essential irrigation systems, leaving the mulberries to wither.

If Buonvicino's white mulberry was the first to be planted in Italy, it was eventually to become the tree of choice for Western sericulture, as it had been in China for millennia. Towards the end of the fifteenth century, the Duke of Milan, Ludovico Sforza, called for white mulberries to be planted on a large scale in Lombardy, earning him the nickname 'Il Moro' (after the Latin for mulberry, although it also means the Moor, or dark-faced one). When sericulture expanded into France from around 1443, it was also accompanied by the 'new' *Morus alba*. The black mulberry – established since the Roman occupation – was retained though, eventually serving only for emergencies, and sometimes during the last week or so before the silkworms spun their cocoons, to make the silk thread 'stronger and heavier'.[13]

Il Moro's project seems to have taken root, at least over the long term. By 1840, over 90 per cent of farmland around Como, the capital of Lombardy, had been planted with white mulberries. In 1853

Gathering mulberry leaves for silk, Italy.

the English novelist Wilkie Collins wrote of seeing mulberry trees – perhaps descendants of Il Moro's trees – growing along Lake Maggiore, on the northeastern edge of Lombardy: 'The great snow mountains were far behind us, gently rising hills were on one side, with vines and mulberry trees, and pretty cottages and country houses dotted all about them.'[14]

A New Agricultural Fashion

From the second half of the fifteenth century it became fashionable for the Italian gentry to plant mulberry trees and raise silkworms on their land. Between 1465 and 1478, for example, two marquises of Mantua, Lodovico and Federico Gonzaga, purchased hundreds of young mulberry trees from Tuscany for their estate in Saviola. Around the same time, mulberries were being planted by landowners throughout Piedmont.[15]

Merchants were also caught up in the mania, such as Nello di Francesco, who planted 10,000 mulberries in Siena in 1481. There were also provincial government incentives. Since 1327 landowners in Modena had been required to plant at least three mulberries. The Florentine authorities issued a similar decree in 1441, requiring peasant farmers to plant between three and fifty mulberries every year. The two main areas for growing mulberries in central and northern Italy were first around Lucca in Tuscany and Bologna in Emilia and second in the Po Valley; the Romagna and the Marches joined in later. Some peasant farmers felt that growing mulberries was much easier and surer than raising sheep, which could be stolen by soldiers or eaten by wolves. With the silkworms hatching in June, sericulture also provided them with an income while waiting to harvest their summer crops.

At one point the Venetian authorities, jealous of competition from other states, refused to allow the export of mulberry saplings. But this did not stop thieves carrying them off in the night – despite the penalty, if caught, of losing an eye or being flogged, dragged through the town and branded. In the sixteenth century, the whole of the Vicenza region seemed to have more mulberry trees than any other species. From an estimated annual production of raw silk in 1504 of 60,000 light pounds, Vicenza's output had doubled to 120,000 light pounds a century later.

Business was, indeed, booming – by the middle of the sixteenth century Italian silk made up 30 per cent of all French imports and about 20 per cent of imports to the Low Countries. By this time, the white mulberry was well established as the primary source of leaves for sericulture throughout Italy, even if black mulberry trees survived as a source of fruit, and as back-up. Furthermore, in an age before chainsaws, it was probably too much work to hack down a rock-hard, old mulberry, so why not leave it standing and benefit from its fruit and shade?

Across the Alps to France

A gentleman soldier, Guy-Pape de Saint-Auban, is credited with planting the first white mulberry in France. Saint-Auban accompanied the 24-year-old Charles VIII on his conquest of Naples, in 1494. With encouragement from the young king, he brought back some white mulberry trees (presumably cuttings), planting them on his estate at Allan, a fortified village built around a medieval castle just a few kilometres south of Montélimar.[16]

There is some evidence to support this account, although there is confusion over the species. Three hundred years later, in 1802, a Monsieur de la Tour-du-Pin de la Chaux is recorded as having built a wall around a massive, 'ancient and respectable' *black* mulberry, forbidding anyone to pick its leaves.[17] It was apparently still standing in 1810, when the geographer and traveller Barthélemy Faujas de Saint-Fond reported seeing a particularly old mulberry at a farm called Bégude: its 'cavernous trunk was divided into three great branches, partly unproductive, but nevertheless still covered every spring in buds, leaves and fruits'.[18] There is an 'Impasse du Mûrier'

Harvesting mulberry leaves, Italy, 18th century.

in the village of Bégude today, and several old mulberries can still be found in the area, though none as old as this.

Even though Charles VIII distributed mulberries throughout various provinces and gave financial incentives to the silk manufactures of Lyons and Tours, moriculture still didn't catch on. The inherently conservative French farmers were suspicious of the alien tree and the new industry, according to a nineteenth-century account

Olivier de Serres, Seigneur du Pradel, known as 'the father of French sericulture'. Lithograph on wove paper by Jean-François Millet, 1858, after a drawing by Daniel de Serres, Olivier's son. Serres wrote a definitive treatise on sericulture and oversaw the implementation of Henri IV's project to plant thousands of mulberry trees in France.

of the history of sericulture in France: 'Despite the example of Italy, where the mulberry was responsible for its wealth, this tree was initially treated with disdain in France. Is it not often the case with anything that is both eminently useful and novel?'[19]

For Faujas de Saint-Fonds, writing in the nineteenth century, Saint-Auban was the unsung hero of French sericulture, having planted France's first white mulberries at Allan a century earlier. The French silk industry, he estimated, was (at the time of writing) worth over 100 million livres in raw silk and 400 million in industrial silk, which he attributed largely to Saint-Auban: 'You see from this just how much one single man, a friend of agriculture, has brought merit to his country and done it much good without causing any tears to be shed, and this man is hardly known.'[20]

Sericulture slumped under Charles's successor, Louis XII, and France once again began importing its silk and silk thread from Spain and Italy. François I (1494–1547) had another go at reviving the fortunes of French silk, bringing looms and two master weavers, Etienne Turquet and Paul Nariz, from Cherasco, Piedmont, in 1536. In 1540 he granted Lyons a monopoly on imports of raw silk and set up a school to teach young girls weaving skills.

Lyons became a global centre for weaving, known for its damask and velvet, although in the early sixteenth century the industry was still dependent on imported raw silk. Under the rule of Henri II (son of François I) from 1547 to his death in 1559, a genuine French sericulture industry gradually grew up, based on hundreds of small-scale silk farms growing their own mulberry trees. It was Henri II, in 1554, who promulgated the first statutes governing the manufacture of silk. Business was doing so well that in 1548, when he entered Lyons with his wife, Catherine de Médicis, the royal procession included 446 silk dyers dressed in grey and black velvet, trimmed with gold thread.

A Perfect Team

It was during the reign of Henri IV of Navarre (1589–1610) that the planting of mulberry trees for the French silk industry was to get its most significant boost so far. Henri had been raised as a Huguenot Protestant, so he was familiar with silk weaving. He later converted to Catholicism in order to bring an end to France's perpetual religious turmoil, which had culminated a few decades earlier (in 1572) in the St Bartholomew's Day massacre of over 10,000 Huguenots, with Catherine de Médicis portrayed as stepping over the bodies of slaughtered Huguenots outside the Louvre Palace.

Henri IV turned sericulture into a national industry, under the watchful eye of his close friend Olivier de Serres. Born in the Ardèche region, Serres had published recommendations for growing fruit under glass in his celebrated book *Le Théâtre de l'agriculture* (1605). He also included a chapter on sericulture and the cultivation of mulberries.

In 1598, Henri IV promulgated the Edict of Nantes, giving Protestants the freedom to practise their religion free from persecution. The Edict brought peace to the mountainous Cévennes region, where Huguenots had sought refuge – and which had been occupied by sectarian and violent *dragonnades* (soldiers who were billeted in Protestant communities and encouraged to intimidate householders) – allowing their white mulberry terraces and silk cocoon harvests to prosper unimpeded.

In 1599, in an effort to promote sericulture on an even larger scale, Henri asked all landowners to plant white mulberries around their houses. 'No mulberries, no manufacturing industry' was the watchword. To further this project, in 1601 the king had a contract drawn up that promised to supply farmers in parishes around Tours, Paris, Lyons and Orleans with 400,000 mulberry saplings, 500 pounds of mulberry seeds, 125 ounces of silkworm eggs and 8,000 printed copies of instructions for planting and cultivating mulberries, raising silkworms and reeling their cocoons. This was all to be at no cost to the farmer.

Henri followed this up the next year with a royal edict, aimed particularly at the Catholic clergy, requiring each parish of the country to use the seeds, trees and silkworm eggs he had given them to establish a nursery for growing mulberries and a silkworm *magnanerie*. The king also required anyone possessing mulberry trees – 'whether white or black' – to put them in the hands of 'experts' nominated by local officials in order to use their leaves for 'raising silkworms for silk'.[21] This was partly propaganda, to prove that 'the temperature of the air and the goodness of the soil are sufficient to produce Silk: with the same or better strength, brilliance and quality as those that we have acclimatised at great cost in far off places.'[22] Reluctant farmers, especially north of the Loire, had been complaining that the climate in France was not right for growing mulberry trees.

In 1596 an enterprising nurseryman, François Traucat, had already started a nursery for home-grown white mulberry trees in the former Roman city of Nîmes, not far from various centres of silk weaving in Arles and Avignon, and on the edge of the Cévennes. With encouragement from Olivier de Serres, using saplings originally imported from Lombardy, Traucat was reportedly able to grow over four million mulberry saplings to supply Provence, Languedoc and the Cévennes – although this figure seems exaggerated.

The effort did seem to pay off, however, as another French expert on sericulture, John Bonoeil, writing in 1622, remarked (this time for the eyes of recalcitrant farmers in Virginia in North America):

> I have seene by experience in the Countrey of Languedock, Prouence, and in Sevenes, and in the Countrey of Avignon, and in some part of Italy, certaine poore folkes which dwell out of Townes, which have but one house upon an earthen floore, and in it but one roome, where at one end they have their bed, and at the other they dresse their meate, which notwithstanding noulrish Silkewormes in it, in the season of the yeere, at which time they prepare and set forth a corner of the said cottage to the same effect, according to the quantity of the leaves which they have: And oftentimes they pay for the leaves of a great Mulbery tree, sixe or eyght shillings the yeere, yea and many times the Wormes thrive better in them, then in great Chambers with other men, I meane, for the little quantity of Wormes which such poore people have.[23]

The mulberry tree is still known in Languedoc as *l'aubre d'aur* (*l'arbre d'or*, or golden tree), mainly because it contributed so much to the prosperity of the region through sericulture.[24]

Mulberries in the Centre of Paris

To set the example, when Henri moved his court from Tours back to Paris in 1601, Serres planted 15–20,000 white mulberry trees 'in diverse places' in the Tuileries gardens, next to his Louvre Palace. This included a double row of trees along the north side of the garden

LE PLAN DE LA VILLE, CITE, VN
Porte S. Antoine
La place Royalle
R. S. Antoine
Marete du Temple
Les Halles
Les marez
le Palmail
Ceste ville est un autre monde
Dedans un monde florissant,
En peuples et en biens puissant
Qui de toutes choses abonde.
Mathæus Mérian. Basiliensis. Fecit 1615

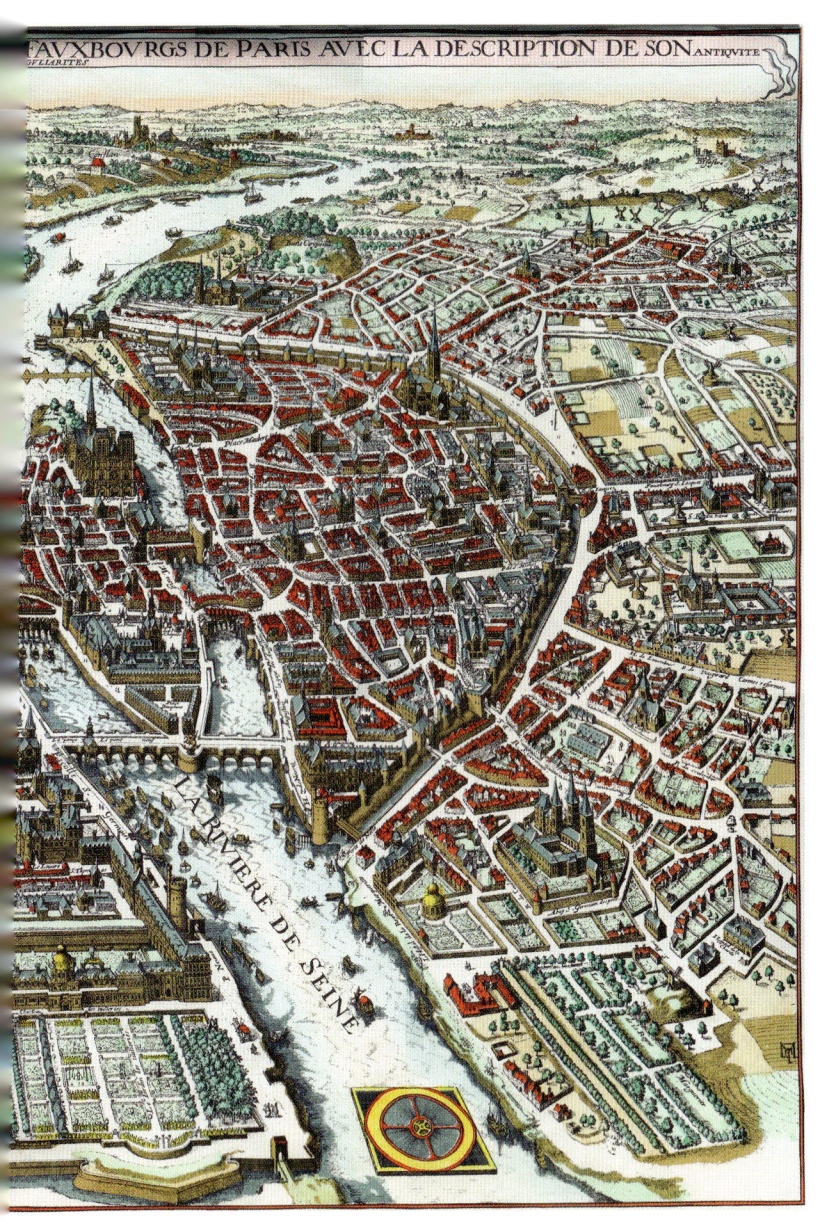

Matthäus Merian's 1615 map of Paris showing the Tuileries gardens at the Louvre (bottom centre). The double row of trees on the left (that is, north) of the gardens are probably white mulberries planted by Olivier de Serres for Henri IV.

(now the rue de Rivoli). He also built a substantial *magnanerie* (silkworm house) on the site. Three years later, the trees had grown tall enough to offer a shaded walk for visitors to the palace. The king liked to admire the trees on after-dinner strolls, when he would sometimes visit his silkworm house and talk to the workers. The young mulberry trees yielded further cuttings, which provided several thousand more mulberry trees around Paris.[25]

In 1610 Henri IV was assassinated by a Catholic fanatic, having escaped as many as twelve previous attempts on his life. His son and nine-year-old heir, Louis XIII, neglected his father's sericulture heritage, even though, ironically, he and his regent mother (Marie de Médicis) were particularly fond of parading in the finest silks, most of them made on French looms. Louis XIII was much more interested in hunting in the forests around Versailles, where he built a hunting lodge – later to become the Palace of Versailles. His father's Tuileries *magnanerie* fell into disuse and the mulberries soon disappeared. Across France, mulberries and sericulture became neglected once more, with the increasingly successful French silk-weaving industry having to import most of its raw silk again.

Before the death of Henri IV, Serres had identified the nearby royal mansions of 'Madrid and Vicenes Wood' as 'very capable to receive three hundred thousand Mulberries'.[26] The Château de Madrid was in Neuilly (adjacent to the Bois de Boulogne to the west of Paris), while the Château de Vincennes was (and still is) about the same distance to the east, just on the outskirts of the city. It is not clear whether Madrid and Vincennes ever received their mulberry plantations, but it seems likely.

Henri's son Louis XIII continued to use the Château de Madrid, but when his son Louis XIV came to the throne (in 1643) and later built himself a palace at Versailles, he abandoned it. In 1656 Louis granted letters patent to Jean Hindret to use the Madrid palace to open the first silk stocking factory in France. It briefly held the monopoly until the 1660s, when stiff competition from Lyons, Nîmes and other silk centres got in on the act, in defiance of Hindret's royal patent. Was the factory opened because of the ready supply of local silk from a mulberry plantation?

In 1836, about 10,000 white mulberries were recorded as growing in Neuilly (where the Château de Madrid had been), about 3,000 of them the *Morus alba multicaulis* variety that was to become so important for the global silk industry. As this variety was unknown in France until 1821, as we shall see, this was probably a new nineteenth-century plantation, but could have reused an existing seventeenth-century plot.

We know less about Vincennes, but the site was certainly used for sericulture in the nineteenth century. In 1829 a certain Monsieur Combet was recorded as having 40,000 mulberries on land near to Vincennes.[27] That town and the neighbouring Saint-Maur still have several districts and a large school that include *mûriers* (mulberries) in their name. Today, though, the silk industries of both Neuilly (Madrid) and Vincennes, along with their mulberry plantations, have long been forgotten, buried under suburban developments.

Mulberries Cross the Atlantic

State-sponsored sericulture continued on both sides of the Channel during the seventeenth century and into the eighteenth century. But, while James I's sericulture project was dragging its heels at home, the king saw an opportunity opening up across the Atlantic in his new colony of Virginia, which then extended from what is now the Canadian border to Florida along the east coast. In the first years of the colony, the Virginia Company was running a successful economy based on the new crop of tobacco – cultivated from a South American seed originally planted by John Rolfe, husband of the Native American princess Pocahontas.

Vehemently opposed to 'the vile custom of Tobacco taking', having published a pamphlet against the habit in 1604,[28] James I sought to encourage colonial farmers to abandon this crop and to plant mulberries instead, under the direction of none other than John Bonoeil (or Bonnell), who, with his wife Francis, had become keeper of the Royal Gardens, Vines and Silkworms at Oatlands after William Stallenge. Like Stallenge, Bonoeil wrote a treatise on the silkworm and mulberries, also using Letellier's 1603 illustrations. In a preface to Bonoeil's pamphlet, James I calls upon 'Adventurers and Planters' to 'use all possible diligence in breeding Silkewormes, and erecting Silkeworkes, and that they rather bestow their travell in compassing this rich and solid Commodity, then in that of Tobacco; which besides much unnecessary expence, brings with it many disorders and inconveniences'.[29]

Bonoeil was particularly struck by the presence of the native red mulberry (*Morus rubra*) growing 'in aboundance naturally' in Virginia. He thought this augured well for the introduction of the silkworm, compared to other places, including France and England, where mulberry trees had had to be introduced. He even writes later about erecting silkworm houses in forests with mulberries, and chopping down the native pines, suggesting that the silk project would at first use the endemic *M. rubra*, rather than the white mulberries that were later introduced. A French vineyard expert on a reconnaissance visit described these red mulberries as 'the tallest and broadest that ever they saw in any Country'.[30]

Having tried unsuccessfully to use *M. rubra* for sericulture, the Virginia Company soon switched to planting white mulberries, this time on a large scale. To encourage farmers to take up sericulture, a system of fines and bounties was introduced. In 1623 a Virginia farmer could be fined 10 livres if he did not plant at least ten mulberry trees for every 40 hectares (100 ac) of land he owned. In 1657 farmers were offered 4,535 kilograms (10,000 lb) of tobacco for every 200 livres' worth of silk they produced.[31] One settler, Sir Robert Murray, planted over 10,000 white mulberries and found a way to produce low hedges or bushes quickly from seed. By 1725, sericulture had started in Pennsylvania and in 1732 it was tried in Georgia.[32]

The Georgian silk industry was slow to take off, with only 1.8 kilograms (4 lb) of fine silk made in 1738, apparently because the supply of fresh mulberry leaves could not meet the demand of

Mulberry Mania

Copy of the Georgia trustee's seal for the establishment of the colony of Georgia (1734–50), one side featuring a mulberry leaf and silkworm, with the motto 'Non Sibi Sed Aliis' (Not for ourselves but for others).

fast-growing silkworms. There were then several successive years of severe spring frosts. By the mid-eighteenth century, though, Savannah (Georgia) had become a leading centre for silk production, under the expert guidance of an Italian from Piedmont, Nicholas Amaris, who planted thousands of mulberry trees.[33] In 1759, the silk-reeling mill in Savannah received 4,535 kilograms (10,000 lb) of home-grown raw silk cocoons. Savannah silk farms even exported silk to England. In 1776 an English botanist, William Bartram, described seeing a large orchard of 'European mulberries' (*M. alba*) growing there.[34] A silkworm cocoon and mulberry leaf were even incorporated into the Savannah seal.[35]

The Carolinas, to the south, and Connecticut, to the north, had also turned to sericulture in the mid-eighteenth century. In 1755 Eliza Lucas Pinckney, an influential Antiguan-born plantation-owner in South Carolina, was able to take enough of her own silk to England to make three dresses, which she presented to the dowager Princess of Wales. But in 1776, the War of Independence dealt a severe blow to American sericulture. This was compounded by the attractions of less labour-intensive crops, such as cotton (for which unskilled slaves could be employed) and rice.

131

The Limitations of State Intervention

While the British monarchy was backing its nascent silk industry in Virginia, Jean-Baptiste Colbert, the minister of finance under Louis XIV (1643–1715), was reviving sericulture (as opposed to just silk weaving) in France. A shrewd financier who had been raised by Italian bankers, Colbert was conscious of the cost of importing raw silk for French weavers in Tours and Lyons, so he set up royal mulberry nurseries in several regions, including Berry, Angoulême, Orléans, Poitou, Maine, Franche-Comté, Burgundy and around Lyons.

The trees were distributed free to farmers – whether they wanted them or not. But the project backfired; the farmers, having neither asked for nor paid for the trees, saw them as more of a nuisance than anything else and let them die. Colbert changed tactic and offered a small reward (24 sous per tree) to anyone whose royal mulberries were still standing after three years. This was more successful, and mulberries soon covered several provinces, notably in the south, especially the Cévennes and Languedoc.

Having at least temporarily sorted out the mulberry problem, Colbert turned his attentions to the manufacture of silk. In 1652 he abolished taxes on silk made in Lyons, while imposing tariffs on imports – including from the neighbouring Comtat Venaissin region. He brought over a highly skilled Italian silk reeler (*fileur*) from Bologna, Pierre Benay, who helped French silk-makers to perfect their skills. Benay was well rewarded for his efforts, both financially and with letters of nobility in France. Meanwhile, back in Italy, his countrymen saw him as a traitor and made effigies of him being hanged. He nevertheless went on to open the first silk mills in Virieu, Isère, which are still there.

But all good things come to an end. For reasons that still divide historians, on 22 October 1685 Louis XIV revoked his grandfather's Edict of Nantes, thus ending the protection of French Protestants from persecution. They were offered the choice of converting to Catholicism or exile – although they were also forbidden from leaving the country, putting them in a double bind. About 300,000 converted, not least to avoid persecution by the *dragonnades*. But around 200,000 still fled, under cover, settling in sympathetic countries.

The Amsterdam authorities built 10,000 houses to accommodate the refugees, while 40–50,000 settled in England, about half of them in the Spitalfields district of London. Although the demographics of Spitalfields have changed dramatically since then – it has welcomed waves of refugees over the centuries – its Huguenot heritage is still very visible in the street names, architecture (former weavers' houses and workshops) as well as several Protestant churches (one now converted into a mosque, having previously been a synagogue). This influx of refugees with silk-weaving skills was too late for James I's own experiment with sericulture in 1609, as we shall see, but it did help provide the expertise for English silk manufacture a hundred years later.

Even though many Huguenot weavers converted to Catholicism under duress and stayed in France, the Edict of Nantes was described by one writer on mulberries, Godefroy Daniel Loffman, as a 'political solecism'.[36] Towards the end of the reign of Louis XIV, very little of the silk thread woven on looms in Lyons was being produced in France. According to one government official writing in 1698, of 6,000 bales of raw silk that entered the city, 1,400 came from the Levant (mostly Persia), 1,600 from Sicily, 1,500 from the rest of Italy, 300 from Spain and just 1,200 from France. Languedoc, Provence and the Dauphiné were the only regions still producing silk thread.[37]

In 1752 the silk weavers of Lyons complained that there were not enough mulberry trees in the region to sustain local sericulture. They asked the controller general to plant them in and around the city, even along main roads and hedgerows. French sericulture was in a sorry state; French raw silk was no longer used for the finest materials, being relegated instead to ribbons, embroidery, trimmings and tapestries, mostly made in Saint-Etienne, a city to the southwest of Lyons. Meanwhile, the English had banned imports of French silks; the Netherlands were opening mills using low-cost raw silk from

Pollarded white mulberries still line country roads in the south of France.

China; and Piedmont had placed a ban on any unwoven silks leaving their territory.

At this time, Prussia was also stealing French workers to start its own industry. Frederick II of Prussia saw sericulture as a path to economic success. In the 1740s, he ordered garrison towns to plant mulberry trees. Anyone willing to plant mulberries would be given land and anyone planting over 1,000 trees would get a grant until the trees made a profit. They could also get Italian silkworm eggs free. In an effort to boost the domestic supply of silk from Prussian mulberries, a 1756 decree forbade the import of foreign silk. Once again, the State was the owner and entrepreneur.

In 1763 a distinguished member of the Royal Agricultural Society of Lyons, one Monsieur Thomé, resolved to 'rescue mulberry trees from the degradation they have come to know in our midst and to return them to the distinguished place they deserve'.[38] To this end he published a number of books on the cultivation of mulberries for silk, including an essay on cultivating the white mulberry.[39] This was the first wave of *muromanie* (mulberry mania) in France. One of Thomé's ambitions – which ended in failure – was to prove that silkworms could be raised on the tree, in the open air, as they used to be in China.

Lyons had recuperated much of Avignon's silk trade, which had been blighted by the plague in 1722–3. But seventy years later, the ongoing French Revolution put an end to this short-lived revival. In 1793, wrote one nineteenth-century Lyons historian,

> a worse disaster than the plague befell our city. All the looms were broken, the silkworks were burned or shut down; humble workers were chased out of their workshops, in order to demolish the pompous edifices that had become the symbol of the opulence of Lyons, the fruit of its manufacturing industry.[40]

One of the revolutionaries caught up in the action – costing him his life – was none other than Roland de la Platrière, who had written so eloquently on the mulberry just a few years before. French mulberry mania was over. No one in the Lyons region was rearing silkworms and most of the still-young mulberry trees that Thomé had planted were grubbed out or neglected.

Marvellous *multicaulis*

In the early nineteenth century, sericulture outside of Asia was to get a massive boost with the introduction of a newly introduced species of white mulberry. It was fast-growing and could produce two or even three flushes of leaves a year, potentially doubling or tripling the income for a farmer. This new variety of white mulberry, *Morus alba multicaulis*, was discovered in 1821 by a French botanist, Georges Guerrard-Samuel Perrottet, in the garden of a Chinese cultivator on the banks of the Pasig river in Manila, the Philippines.[41] The Philippines were on a regular trading route for ships sailing out of Chinese ports. The tree had long been favoured by the Chinese and was to revolutionize sericulture across the globe.

Known as the *Lu sang* mulberry in China – where it is now widely cultivated in the Jiangsu, Shaanxi, Sichuan and Zhejiang provinces – this species produces more abundant foliage than the common white mulberry and is easily propagated from cuttings and layers. It can also be grown quickly from seed. The original Perrottet variety has huge, bowl-shaped, crinkly leaves – up to 30 centimetres (12 in.) wide and 38 centimetres (15 in.) long – and can produce two flushes of foliage in the same year, under the right conditions. The variety that was widely propagated in the West, though, has large, flat leaves that are not puckered. *M. multicaulis* responds well to heavy pruning, meaning that it can be grown as a low bush, making it easy to harvest the leaves. According to Perrottet, this means that 'a child is sufficient for gathering the food of a large establishment of silk worms.' An added bonus of *M. multicaulis* is that it produces long, black fruit that taste good.

The mulberries described by Robert Fortune in Huzhou in the 1850s were probably *multicaulis* (*Lu sang*):

> The variety of mulberry cultivated in this district appears to be quite distinct from that which is grown in the southern parts of China and in the silk districts of India. Its leaves are much larger, more glossy, and have more firmness and substance than any other variety which has come to my notice . . . This variety is not reproduced from seed, and hence all the plantations are formed of grafted trees. Each plant is grafted from a foot to two feet above the ground, and rarely

higher. The trees are planted in rows from five to six feet apart, and are allowed to grow from six to ten feet high only, for the convenience of gathering the leaves . . . When the bushes have attained their full size the young shoots with the leaves are clipped close off by the stumps, and shoots and leaves carried home together to the farm-yard to be plucked and prepared for the worms.[42]

In the early nineteenth century, when M. *multicaulis* became known outside of China, it stimulated something of a craze on both sides of the Atlantic. In France, the Count of Marnezia, prefect of the Rhône district, replanted white mulberries around Lyons and reopened the *magnaneries* in the surrounding countryside. By 1824 the looms of Lyons were once again working day and night 'to the delight of our ears'.[43] From 4,000 working looms in Lyons in 1699, the number had rocketed to 24,000 in 1824, two-thirds of them within the city walls. The first half of the nineteenth century was also when extensive mulberry plantations were established in Vincennes and Neuilly, just outside Paris, as we saw earlier in this chapter.

Across the Atlantic in New England, a nurseryman, Samuel Whitmarsh, fanned the flames of a sudden demand for M. *multicaulis* slips in 1823 by exaggerating the immediate rewards they would bring to anyone who planted them for sericulture. Demand quickly outstripped supply, with prices shooting up from 10 cents a tree in 1835 to nearly $1 a tree by 1838. People were even speculating on the trees, buying and selling them to make a profit with no intention of ever using them to feed silkworms.

Meanwhile, the Levant, with its long history of silk manufacture stretching back over 1,000 years, also enjoyed the nineteenth-century boom in sericulture. The Cornish biblical scholar John Kitto, on a visit to Palestine and Lebanon around 1840, found mulberries being grown for silk both on a small scale, in the courtyards and gardens of houses, as well as in extensive plantations and narrow mountain terraces:

The mulberry tree is the source of wealth to the whole country of the Druzes, by the quantities of silk which it enables them to produce. Throughout the mountains of Lebanon and Kesroun, and in the plain below, the mulberry-tree is, for this reason, most extensively cultivated; and as the price of silk, the staple commodity of the district, has doubled within the last twelve years, the cultivation is increasing, in some places to the exclusion of every other tree, and even to the neglect of garden produce, which it is found cheaper to purchase from places which have not the same inducements to forego the culture.[44]

Sericulture, most likely based on *M. multicaulis*, also flourished in Greece during the nineteenth century – an important silk-producing centre in the Byzantine Empire 1,000 years earlier, but using the local *M. nigra*. Edward Joy Morris, better known as a master builder of wooden carousels in Philadelphia, reported seeing plantations of mulberries in his travels through Sparta in the 1840s;[45] and in the 1950s Arnold Krochmal, an American professor of agriculture, found 112,000 pollarded white mulberry trees, which he estimated to be over 150 years old, still growing outside the village of Basilica in Macedonia, northern Greece. Farming families continued to practise sericulture there, but he predicted that the end was not far off. 'At the present rate of disappearance,' he wrote, 'the mulberry tree will vanish from northern Greece as a crop within ten or 15 years, and only a few solitary survivors will stand to mark the spot where once they grew in thousands.'[46]

Pébrine and the Orphaned Mulberries

The nineteenth-century boom in Western sericulture – which had been eclipsing Asian silk exports – was not to last long. In America it soon became clear that the claims for *M. multicaulis* were harder to achieve than farmers had been led to believe. According to Patrick

Mulberry Mania

Advertisement for the *Silk Grower* magazine showing giant *Morus multicaulis* leaf grown by the Cheney brothers. c. 1870.

Skahill, writing on the celebrated Cheney Bros silk company of Connecticut,

> investors simply stopped giving money to the silk 'experiment.' Mulberry farms disappeared and by 1840 the silk speculation bubble had entirely burst. Mulberry trees were sold as pea brush (branches and twigs, usually prunings, used as supports for pea plants) or simply burned by farmers unable to push the worthless crop.[47]

Prices for *M. multicaulis* crashed below Whitmarsh's original 10 cents. Farmers turned back to other, more familiar crops, like cotton and tobacco.

Cheney Bros saw this coming, however, and switched from sericulture and raw silk production to weaving raw silk. Their Manchester

(Connecticut) silk mill became so successful that it spawned a whole town, Cheney Village, with its own water, sewage and electricity works, railways, schools and recreation facilities. In 1923 it turned over $23 million in sales. But the 1929 Wall Street stock market crash, compounded by a later zeal for the new synthetic fibres, forced the company to sell off its assets and diversify. It finally went into liquidation in 1978. The fifteen-block village, with its mansions, factories and workers' housing, became a national museum.

The *coup de grâce* for sericulture in the West came with the outbreak of *pébrine* (pepper disease) in 1845, a parasitic disease that affects the silkworm and stops it spinning an adequate cocoon, causing it to die. In both France and Italy, sericulture was a cottage industry, with silkworms being raised in cramped, unhygienic conditions. The French microbiologist Louis Pasteur soon found a means to prevent the *pébrine* epidemic from spreading further, essentially by destroying diseased colonies of silkworms and improving hygiene in the silkworm houses. But by then both French and Italian sericulture had virtually collapsed.[48] In 1840, France had produced 26,000 tonnes of silk. By 1865 the output had plummeted to 4,000 tonnes. With no silkworms to nourish, hundreds of thousands of mulberry trees became, essentially, orphaned, with little *raison d'être*.

The early industrial revolution in Britain, together with the availability of cheap manpower in the British Empire in Bengal and India, further undermined French and Italian exports, in what may have been the first effects of globalization. Not only did the new industrial looms of the Lombard brothers' silk mills in Derbyshire, in the English Midlands, revolutionize the production of silk, but mulberry plantations in Bengal could sustain the supply of raw silk, even if Italian silk was still of better quality. Between 1780 and 1830, over half of raw silk imports to Britain came from Bengal.[49]

The European sericulture crisis did not sound the death knell for everyone, though. Turkish peasant farmers turned the *pébrine* epidemic into an opportunity. Turkey had had a flourishing silk-weaving industry since the Byzantine era and started producing its own silk in the late sixteenth century, centred around the port city of Bursa and in small farms scattered across the country. Gradually, though, silk weaving gave way to simply exporting raw silk.

When Turkish silk farmers were hit by *pébrine*, unlike in France and Italy, they showed remarkable ingenuity in spotting a new market opening, just as it was proving difficult to compete with new, cheap Asian silk imports. As the epidemic affected silkworms and not mulberries, farmers began harvesting, drying and commercializing the fruit, notably of *M. alba*. Later, when the *pébrine* outbreak had been stemmed, a few farmers returned to raising silk moths again, but this time to harvest and export their eggs (or 'seeds').

The Spectacular Rise of Japanese Sericulture

The decline of sericulture in the West during the nineteenth century was paralleled – if not precipitated – by a spectacular rise in silk manufacture in Japan. Although the Japanese had been making silk since the third century BCE, the country had remained economically isolated until the arrival of Admiral Matthew Perry from the U.S. in 1859 and the signing of new international trade treaties. The opening of the Suez Canal in 1872 gave Japanese silk a further boost, offering a faster and more economical supply route to Europe. Japan also modernized quickly, introducing the latest reeling technology from France. This was in France's interest as it could not meet its own demands for raw silk domestically. The Tomioka silk mill in Gunma Prefecture opened in 1872 and came to symbolize Japan's entry into the industrial world.

Although the European *pébrine* outbreak has often been blamed for allowing Japanese sericulture to blossom, the picture is in fact much more subtle. *Pébrine* was also endemic to Japan, but different practices of cultivating mulberries and rearing silkworms meant that the disease was more easily contained there. In contrast to the poor hygiene that characterized European sericulture, the Japanese women responsible for rearing silkworms followed a strict code of practice,

Japanese workers inspecting silk cocoons, within view of Mount Fuji (southwest of Tokyo). Photograph by Italian photographer Felice Beato and hand-coloured by local Japanese watercolour artists. Beato was one of the first Western photographers to be allowed to travel around the previously closed country. From Charles Arthur Sheffeld, *Silk: Its Origin, Culture, and Manufacture* (1911).

changing their clothes several times a day and washing their hands frequently. They even spoke in hushed voices, so as not to upset the silkworms.[50] Japanese silk farmers adopted the Chinese technique of feeding silkworms on finely chopped fresh white mulberry leaves. The size of the chopped pieces was gradually increased as the larvae developed, until the final stages before pupation, when the silkworms were placed directly onto mulberry twigs to feed on whole leaves. This practice seems to have enabled the silkworms to grow at a faster rate and with lower mortality.

Land for mulberry cultivation was also limited in Japan, but the climatic conditions and the practice of pruning the trees close to the ground meant that it was possible to have two or even three harvests of leaves a year. As Claudio Zanier has pointed out, while the size of the (white) mulberry trees being widely cultivated in both Japan and Italy decreased through pollarding, to make the leaves easier to pick, the climatic conditions in Italy, especially in the south, did not allow small mulberry trees exfoliated in the spring to produce a second flush by late summer, so only one harvest was possible.[51]

Despite an interruption to trade precipitated by the Second World War and the arrival on the Western market of synthetic fibres like rayon and nylon, Japan dominated the world market for raw silk in terms of production and export for most of the twentieth century until the early 1970s, with a 60–80 per cent market share. As many as 40 per cent of Japanese farmers were employed in sericulture in the 1930s, a figure that rose to 70 per cent in provinces like Gunma.

As has been the story of every country to invest heavily in sericulture, though, the tide was to turn for Japan, too. A combination of factors, including the U.S.'s freezing of Japanese assets during the 1940s, led to the decline of the Japanese raw silk industry. The Tomioka silk mill closed but the factory site was preserved as a museum and inscribed on the UNESCO World Heritage List in 2014.

Gathering mulberry leaves to feed silkworms at Yamagata Kenritsu Shonai Agriculture High School in Tsuruoka, Japan. Vintage postcard, probably c. 1947, when the school was opened.

With the decline in Japanese sericulture China once again established its global dominance, gaining 70 per cent of the export market. Today, only around 14,500 hectares (35,830 ac) of land are devoted to mulberry cultivation in Japan, with around 1,700 hectares (4,200 ac) using intense, highly mechanized harvesting. The mulberry trees are coppiced so that they remain low shrubs, with as many as 2,500 plants for every 10 hectares (25 ac).

National sericulture projects, however, have a tendency to spring back up again even when everyone thinks they are dead. In 2017 Japan's Kumamoto prefecture opened a U.S.$21 million 'bioclean' silkworm factory in what it is calling 'Silk on Valley'. Around 80,000 mulberries have been planted in 'sky mulberry fields' at altitudes of 600 metres (1,970 ft) in the surrounding mountains. The mulberries will be kept as low bushes in 100-metre-long (328-ft) rows that can each be mechanically harvested in just five minutes. Rather than feed the silkworms whole leaves, they will be dried, mashed and mixed with other ingredients. However, an earlier attempt in the 1980s–90s to use non-mulberry artificial feed failed.[52]

The Great Mulberry of Usune, Numata, Gunma, Japan, 2018.

Modern mulberry plantation in Fukuoka, Kyushu, Japan, 2015.

Full Circle

As Japanese dominance subsided during and immediately after the Second World War, China gradually regained its position as world leader in the production of silk cocoons. Even though new technology had been introduced from Europe, many producers were still reeling silk by hand. Surprisingly, this was just as productive as industrial filature, even if the consistency was more variable.[53] By 1998, around 626,000 hectares (1,547,000 ac) of land were under mulberry cultivation in China, followed by around 280,000 hectares (692,000 ac) in India, the second largest producer of silk cocoons. Sericulture based on the white mulberry had gone full circle.

The large-scale planting of mulberries in Europe and most of Central Asia had come to an end. Françoise Clavairolle reports desperate eye-witness accounts of the social decimation this caused in the Cévennes region of France as skills faded, mulberry terraces became neglected and overgrown, and the *magnanerie* silkworm houses were sold as second homes, gîtes and boutique hotels.[54] But the mulberry migration has not stopped. The UN Food and Agriculture Organization is actively promoting mulberry leaves as fodder for cattle in developing countries in the southern hemisphere. As one 2,000-year chapter in the mulberry's peregrinations closes, another opens.

five
Art, Legend and Literature

꒰

The oldest myths that have grown up around the mulberry tree originate in ancient China, where the white mulberry became an almost magical source of wealth some 4,000 years ago, through sericulture. Other myths derive from the notorious, staining, blood-red juice of the black mulberry fruit. As mulberry trees came to dominate the landscapes of parts of Central Asia, the Middle East and countries around the Mediterranean, they began to figure in the poetry and literature of these places: raising silkworms as a hobby or a commercial activity has featured in the work of novelists such as Virginia Woolf and Jeffrey Eugenides, with mulberry leaves sneaking in as part of the narrative.

The Mulberry in Ancient Chinese Mythology

The legend of Princess Leizu, the first sericulturalist, grew up to account for the discovery of silk and sericulture around 2700 BCE, as we have seen. The mulberry tree also plays a central role in several other Chinese legends, recently brought together by sinologists. In particular, as gods and demigods in Chinese mythology metamorphose easily between divine and human forms, as Anne Birrell explains, the mulberry tree often acts as an *axis mundi* providing a pathway between heaven and Earth.[1]

The Silkworm Horse

The myth of the silkworm horse recounts the origin of the mulberry tree itself. In this story, which was first written down in a fourth-century collection known as *Soushen Ji* (In Search of the Supernatural), a young girl, Can Nü, is left alone with a stallion while her father is away.[2] Afraid that the girl's father has been killed, Can Nü's mother promises that she will give her daughter away to the first person who brings him back home. Enchanted by this prospect, the horse races off, finds Nü's father and persuades him to come home. When her father learns about the promise, he is angry that such a peculiar marriage would bring shame upon his family. So, he kills the horse, leaving the skin to dry, before leaving once again on his travels.

No sooner has he left than the skin flies up into the air, wraps around Can Nü and carries her off. When the girl's father finally returns home and finds his daughter missing, he asks a neighbour's wife to look for her. After much searching, the neighbour discovers that girl and horse have turned into a silkworm, spinning a cocoon in the branches of a large, old mulberry tree. When unravelled, the cocoon produces the thickest and longest silk thread ever spun. The neighbour vows to care for the tree, and calls it *sang* (which means to weep or mourn in Mandarin).

The Hollow Mulberry

The myth of the hollow mulberry (*Kong sang*) is associated with Yi Yin, first minister to Tang, the founder of the Shang dynasty (1766–1753 BCE).[3] Yi Yin helped Tang to defeat a tyrannical ruler. Although the hollow mulberry is a cosmic tree (another *axis mundi*), some scholars believe that *Kong sang* was a real place, possibly on a mountain in the north or east of China.[4] While Confucius is said to have been born under the hollow mulberry, the myth, as recounted in the *Annals of Master Lu* (third century BCE; *Lüshi chunqiu*), describes it as the birthplace of Yi Yin.[5]

Wu liang shrine relief depicting Xihe, Yi and *Fu sang* tree, in Édouard Chavannes, *Mission archéologique dans la Chine septentrionale*, vol. III (Archaeological Mission to Northern China, 1909).

According to the myth, a woman living near the river Yi becomes pregnant. In a dream a spirit tells her that if her mortar bowl leaks water, she should immediately go as far away as possible, to the east – but be careful not to look back. When she awakes the next morning, she notices that her mortar bowl is, indeed, leaking, so she picks up a few belongings and hurries ten leagues to the east. Forgetting what the spirit had told her, she turns to take a last look at her village, only to see that it has been flooded. No sooner has she witnessed the tragedy of the flood, when her body turns into a hollow mulberry tree. Some months later, a girl is out picking mulberry leaves when

Hou Yi, as depicted in Xiao Yuncong's illustrated *Inquiry of the Heavens* (1645).

she finds a baby in the hollow tree. She takes it to her master, who allows it to be raised as his own son. The baby is Yi Yin. In this story, the hollow mulberry is literally the womb.

The Leaning Mulberry, Hou Yi and the Ten Suns

Perhaps the most celebrated of the mulberry myths is that of *Fu sang*, the leaning mulberry tree. This is a massive, 91-metre-high (300-ft) gnarled mulberry tree growing in the east, near Tang Valley (sometimes translated as Warm Springs Valley). Ten suns perch in the branches of the tree, each corresponding to one day of a ten-day week. At the beginning of each new day, one sun rises to the top of the tree, then takes off, travelling slowly across the sky to the Kunlun Mountains in the west, where it comes to rest in another tree, called the *Ruomu* or *Ruo* tree. In some versions of the myth, the sun then dies, only to be reborn ten days later in the *Fu sang* tree. In another version, the sun travels back to the east by an underground river that connects the *Fu sang* tree with the *Ruomu* tree, in time for the next cycle. According to sinologist Sarah Allan, this river could be the same as the Yellow Spring (*Huang Qan*), a watery underworld that comes to the surface at the root of the *Ruo* and *Fu sang* trees.[6]

The suns are ten brothers, all sons of the god Dijun, and are often depicted as black three-legged ravens or crows. In some images, the ravens carry the suns across the heavens; in others the ravens are inside the suns, and in yet others, the ravens stand for the suns – they *are* the suns.[7] The myth of the *Fu sang* tree is often linked to the legend of Hou Yi, or Archer Yi, a divine warrior. One day, during the time of a wise king, Yao-no, all ten suns rise together, causing a terrible drought, scorching the earth and burning plant life. Dijun asks Hou Yi to go down to Earth to save the world. At first, Hou Yi tries just to scare the suns, but when this does not work he takes aim and shoots down the first sun (son), which plummets to Earth as a red-hot fireball in a shower of golden raven's feathers. One by one, he shoots down eight more of the remaining suns. He cannot shoot down the 'true' sun for that day, but leaves it to provide the light and warmth needed for life on Earth.

While the people are grateful to Hou Yi, Dijun is angry at the loss of his sons, and banishes Hou Yi from the realm of the gods. Feeling lonely on Earth, Hou Yi takes a wife, the beautiful Chang'e. He can't bear the thought that death will one day separate them, so goes to the top of the Jade Mountain to ask the Queen of the West for help. She gives him a chalice containing a magic potion that will allow him to rise straight up to heaven the moment he dies. But Chang'e yearns for immortality, so steals the chalice and drinks the potion. She immediately flies up to heaven and takes up residence in the moon. Poor Hou Yi is left to live out his life on Earth alone.[8]

Things don't work out so well for Chang'e either, though. As soon as she arrives in the moon she turns into a striped toad (*Chanchu*). Chang'e, the moon goddess, is still celebrated in China on the Mid-Autumn Festival, a full-moon day roughly coinciding with the autumn equinox (September–October).

The *Fu sang* and Hou Yi myth is thought to date back to the Shang period, and might evoke a real drought that occurred at the start of the dynasty and lasted for five years, while Hou Yi was also a real-life tribal leader in ancient China.[9] The myth was still alive in the Han period (206 BCE–220 CE) and is depicted on a western Han dynasty funerary pendant, excavated in 1972 from a tomb at the Mawangdui site (Hunan Province). The pendant shows nine suns in the branches of a twisted tree. A moon in one corner contains a toad. The myth is also depicted on tomb murals discovered in Hunan, while bronze trees found at the Sanxingdui site might also be *Fu sang* trees.[10] It is interesting that *Fu sang* is described as both leaning and having a twisted trunk, which are typical features of the black mulberry (*Morus nigra*), but not of the common Chinese white mulberry (*Morus alba*).

As *Fu sang* is associated with the rising sun, some scholars have speculated that it might refer to an island in the east, possibly Japan. In much more recent times, Hou Yi has been used as the model for a warrior hero in the *Smite* video game.

Mulberry in the I Ching

The pre-Confucian divinatory text, the *I Ching* (*Yijing*), or *Book of Changes*, uses the image of the mulberry in the interpretation of the twelfth of its 64 hexagrams, *Pi, Standstill* (Stagnation):

> Standstill is giving way,
> Good fortune for the great man.
> 'What if it should fail, what if it should fail?'
> In this way he ties it to a cluster of mulberry shoots.

The German sinologist Richard Wilhelm, who devoted much of his working life to translating and interpreting the *I Ching*, adds this explanation: 'when a mulberry bush is cut down, a number of unusually strong shoots sprout from the roots. Hence the image of tying something to a cluster of mulberry shoots is used to symbolize the way of making success certain.'[11]

Blood and Tragedy

The staining, blood-red juice of black mulberry fruit – what Virgil called *sanguinea morus* – has fired up the imagination of writers throughout history, often with negative or gory associations. One example from antiquity comes to us via the Greco-Roman biographer and essayist Lucius Plutarchus (Plutarch, 45–127 CE). According to Plutarch, an Athenian poet once described the face of the dictator Lucius Cornelius Sulla as 'a mulberry sprinkled o'er with meal' to conjure up his 'fearsome face covered in red blotches spotted with white'.[12]

The Murder of Thomas Becket

A thousand years later, a black mulberry tree was linked to the bloody assassination of Thomas Becket, Archbishop of Canterbury during the reign of Henry II of England (1154–89 CE). An Englishman, born and educated in France, Becket was a young high-flyer who soon came to the attention of the king. The two became close: Henry first made Becket chancellor, then soon afterwards Archbishop of Canterbury, hoping thereby to gain greater control over the Church, to the detriment of the pope. Once in post, however, Becket switched allegiance to the pope, greatly angering the king, who offered a reward for anyone who got rid of his renegade friend.

According to Gervase, a monk at Canterbury cathedral, four knights apparently took up the challenge, hacking Becket to death while he was kneeling at the altar:

> on the fifth day of the nativity, which was the third day of the week, there arrived four courtiers, who desired to speak with the archbishop, thinking by this to discover the weak points [of the monastery]. These were Reginald Fitz-Urse, Hugh de Morville, William de Traci, and Richard Brito. After a long discussion, they began to employ threats; and at length rising up hastily, they went out into the courtyard; and under the spreading branches of a mulberry-tree, they cast off the garments with which they had covered their breastplates, and, accompanied by those persons whom they had summoned from the province, they returned into the archbishop's palace ... Having entered the church, he [Becket] paused at the threshold; and he asked his attendants of what they were afraid. When the clerks began to fall into disorder, he said, 'Depart, ye cowards! Let these blind madmen go on in their career. We command you, in virtue of your obedience, not to shut the door.'
>
> While he was thus speaking, behold! the executioners having ransacked the bishop's palace, rushed together through the cloisters; three of whom carried hatchets in their left hands, and one an axe or a two-edged glaive, while all of them brandished drawn swords in their right hands.[13]

I will spare the reader the gruesome details that follow.

Pyramus and Thisbe

Perhaps the most famous tale associated with the (black) mulberry is that of the ill-fated lovers Pyramus and Thisbe. In Book IV of his *Metamorphoses*, the Latin author Ovid, writing at the end of the first century BCE, tells how the handsome Pyramus and the beautiful Thisbe lived next door to each other. Although they were deeply in love, their parents were unhappy with the match and would not allow them to marry. The lovers used to whisper to each other through a crack in the wall between their two houses and one day decided to elope, arranging to meet secretly at night under a mulberry tree.

When Thisbe arrived at the rendezvous she disturbed a lioness, whose jaws were dripping with blood from a young deer it had just killed. Frightened by the fierce beast, Thisbe ran off, dropping her white veil in her haste. The lioness sniffed at the veil, shaking it violently in frustration at being interrupted in its meal. Pyramus arrived at the tree a few minutes later, finding the bloodstained veil of his beloved under the tree. Seeing the lioness slinking off into the bushes he immediately thought that the beast must have killed her. Broken-hearted, he unsheathed his sword and took his own life.

A little while later, desperate to find her lover and run away from this dreadful place, Thisbe plucked up the courage to go back to the mulberry tree. Here she found Pyramus dying on the ground, his bloody sword lying beside him. Realizing what had happened, Thisbe took his sword and killed herself – but not before putting a curse on the mulberry tree, turning its white fruit blood-red. And this is exactly what happens every year, as the pale, unripe fruit of the black mulberry gradually turns to a deep, dark red. But Ovid may have been even more perspicacious if the hypothesis that *M. nigra* is a complex and archaic hybrid of two *M. alba* species turns out to be true.

Shakespearean scholar Patricia Parker has found the original Latin version of the tale of Pyramus and Thisbe to be 'bristling with puns' on the Latin word for mulberry (*morus*). These include *amor*

Gregorio Pagani, *Pyramus and Thisbe*, 1558–1605, oil on canvas.

(the love between the young couple), *murmur* (as they whisper through the wall, which is *murus* in Latin), *mors* (their tragic death) and *morus* (delay – the fatal interval between the arrival of the two lovers at the mulberry (*morus*) tree).[14] In some illustrations of the story, Pyramus actually turns into a mulberry tree.

More Puns on 'Morus'

In her fascinating analysis, Parker discusses at length other *morus* puns surrounding Thomas More (1478–1535), Henry VIII's ill-fated chancellor. More was beheaded when he refused to endorse the king's marriage to Anne Boleyn, preferring to honour his deep Catholic faith. More was partial to quipping with his good friend the humanist Dutch philosopher Erasmus in Latin, which was still a lingua franca among the educated in the fifteenth and sixteenth centuries. More planted a black mulberry (*arbor morus*) in the grounds of the house he built by the Thames, in what was then the small village of Chelsea. Today, two old black mulberries and several more recently planted trees still grow in the beautiful gardens of a Catholic seminary on the site of More's former estate. One of them is claimed to be the very tree that More planted, but this is most unlikely, although it could be a descendant.

More and Erasmus had great fun with puns on the root syllable of his name *mor-*, which means 'fool' in Latin. In a dedicatory letter to his *Encomium Moriae* (Praise of Folly), Erasmus tells More why he chose the title for his book, with its deliberate pun on his name: 'In the first place, it was your own family name of More, which is as near to the Greek word for folly, *moria*, as you are far from it in fact, and everyone agrees that you couldn't be farther removed.'[15] Erasmus wrote the book while he was staying at More's house in Chelsea in the summer of 1509 (incidentally when the mulberries on More's tree would have been ripe). In the early seventeenth century, Ludovicus Rumetius, canon of Notre Dame cathedral in Paris, also played on More's name, in a more chilling way: *non mori sanguine, sed Thomae Mori* (blood not of the mulberry but of Thomas More).

The raw material for other puns included 'more' (greater than), morals (*more*), *morosus* (melancholy), memento mori (in remembrance of More's death), Moor (black, as in Shakespeare's Othello). Meanwhile, Archbishop Morton, in whose house More had once served as a young man, had a more-tree (mulberry) issuing from a barrel (tun) as his emblem (More-tun). Finally, the sixteenth-century writer Thomas Stepleton, in his *Tres Thomae* – the triple biography of Thomas the Apostle, Thomas Becket and Thomas More, translated by Parker – writes:

> *Dat fructus homini, Bombyci serica morus*
> *Virtuti, et Sophiae* MORUS *utrumque dabit*
> *Moribus e* MORI *texes tibi serica morum.*
> *Si* MORI *Bombyx sedule, Lector, eris.* (Emphasis by Parker.)

> The mulberry tree [*morus*] gives fruit to man, silk to the silkworm.
> More [*Morus*] will give both to virtue and wisdom.
> From the morals [*mores*] of More [*Mori*] you will weave yourself silken garments of character [*mores*]
> If you, reader, will be an attentive silkworm of this *Morus* or *More*.]

Shakespeare's Mulberries

In the late sixteenth century and early seventeenth century, when William Shakespeare was writing, the only mature mulberries found in England would have been *Morus nigra*, a species reputed for its fruit and shade, the two attributes to which he refers. Shakespeare often drew on the classics, including Ovid's *Metamorphoses*, and wove comic references to Pyramus and Thisbe into the plot for *A Midsummer Night's Dream*. In Act III, Scene I, Titania, queen of the fairies, tells her fairies to be nice to Bottom:

> Be kind and courteous to this gentleman;
> Hop in his walks, and gambol in his eyes;
> Feed him with apricocks and dewberries,
> With purple grapes, green figs, and mulberries;
> The honey bags steal from the bumble bees,

And, for night tapers, crop their waxen thighs,
And light them at the fiery glowworm's eyes
To have my love to bed, and to arise;
And pluck the wings from painted butterflies,
To fan the moonbeams from his sleeping eyes:
Nod to him, elves, and do him courtesies.
(*A Midsummer Night's Dream*, III.1)

Here the mulberry fruit is used as a symbol of sweetness, placed alongside other rare fruit, which, as it happens, were also first introduced to England by the Romans. Although Shakespeare incorporates Ovid's tragedy into the plot, he completely avoids the association of mulberry fruit with gore: again, in his narrative poem *Venus and Adonis* (published in 1593 and also influenced by Ovid), the fruit is intended to conjure up images of ripe lusciousness:

When he beheld his shadow in the brook,
The fishes spread on it their golden gills;
When he was by, the birds such pleasure took
That some would sing, some other in their bills
Would bring him mulberries and ripe-red cherries:
He fed them with his sight, they him with berries.

In his Roman war tragedy, *Coriolanus*, written between 1605 and 1609, it is the fragility of the ripe mulberry that Shakespeare exploits. In Act II, Scene 3, the influential Volumnia appeals to her heroic but arrogant son, Coriolanus, to put his contempt for the people aside and appease them, with a heart that is no longer 'stout', but 'now humble as the ripest mulberry/ That will not hold the handling'.

A claim that Shakespeare became interested in mulberries because of the contemporary vogue surrounding James I's efforts to encourage planting on a wide scale has been discounted, not least because the king's 1607–8 edict came after the playwright had published the works that mention mulberries. *A Midsummer Night's Dream* was published in

1600, and was probably written in 1594 or 1595, over a decade before James's sericulture project. However, Shakespeare may have had direct experience of the fragile mulberry fruit from a tree growing at his New Place house in Stratford-upon-Avon, which he purchased in 1597, and where he lived during the last years of his life. This tree was to cause considerable controversy a century later, as we shall see in the final chapter. Ben Jonson, however, a younger contemporary of Shakespeare, was undoubtedly influenced by this mulberry vogue when he wrote of 'a courtier, that feeds on mulberry leaves, like a true silkworm', in *The Magnetic Lady*, published in 1632.

A mulberry tree also crops up in the ongoing speculation surrounding the identity of the Dark Lady of Shakespeare's sonnets. One thesis is that she came from the wealthy Bassano family of Venetian merchants, whose coat of arms featured a mulberry tree and silk moth, evocative of their origins in Bassano del Grappa, north

Tea caddy surmounted with carving of mulberry leaves and berries, wrongly attributed to Thomas Sharp. Made from wood from Shakespeare's mulberry tree. 18th or 19th century.

Bassano family crest with mulberry tree, leaves and silk moths — or are they bees?

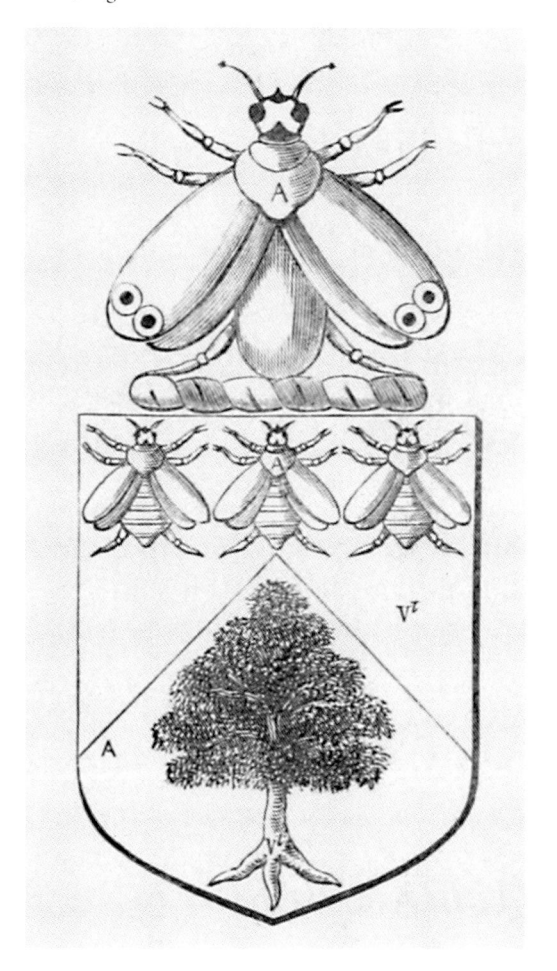

of Venice. A miniature of an unknown lady painted in 1593 by Nicholas Hilliard, entitled Mrs Holland and now in the Victoria and Albert Museum, shows a beautiful woman wearing a bodice decorated with silk moths, stags and mulberry trees, which seems to be of Emilia Bassano (or Amelia Bassano Lanier).[16]

Mulberries in Visual Art

While paper made from the bark of mulberry trees may be highly regarded as a medium for visual artists, the tree and its fruit are not

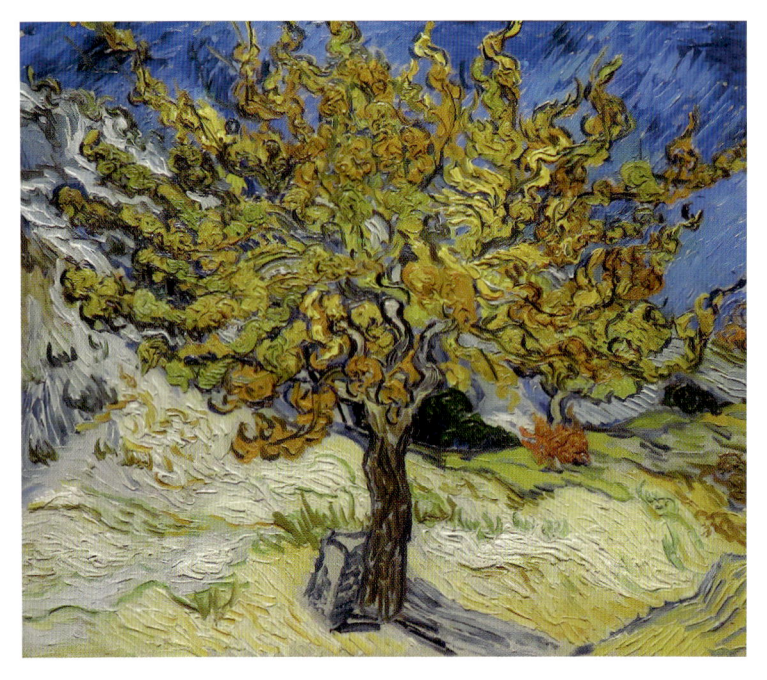

Vincent van Gogh, *The Mulberry Tree*, 1889, oil on canvas.

common subjects. One of the best-known paintings of a mulberry tree was made by Dutch post-Impressionist painter Vincent van Gogh in 1889, a year before his suicide. Made in the autumn, the painting shows what is probably a white mulberry in a rocky landscape against a blue sky. The tree stood in the grounds of the Saint-Paul-de-Mausole psychiatric asylum, a former eleventh-century Romanesque monastery near the town of Saint-Rémy-de-Provence in France. He had admitted himself in May that year after a fight with fellow artist Paul Gauguin, during which Van Gogh lost an ear. The two artists had met in Paris in 1887 and soon became friends, even planning to start a utopian colony of artists in Polynesia. In October 1888, Gauguin joined Van Gogh in rooms Vincent had rented in a house in Arles. But the two argued and, following a violent tussle in the street, Vincent lost his left ear. It has been widely reported that Van Gogh cut off his own ear with a razor after the fight – evidence of his growing madness. A recent thesis has challenged this, though, suggesting

Liang Shaoji, *Beds Nature Series No. 10*, 1993, charred copper, silk, cocoon.

that Gauguin, a skilled fencer, cut off his friend's ear with his epée, either in anger or in self defence.[17] The painting is a wonderful illustration of the bright yellow colour of mulberry leaves in autumn, which earned the tree the sobriquet *arbre d'or* (golden tree) in French. Another painting, *The Garden of Saint-Paul Hospital*, made in December 1889, seems to show other mulberry trees, one of which is old and has lost a limb.

The *Nature* series of Shanghai-based Chinese artist Liang Shaoji does not directly represent mulberries, although they are ever-present. In this work, which he started in 1986, Liang uses the life-cycle of the silkworm as a trope to express time, the fourth dimension. The

Jess Shepherd, *040420161613 Mulberry (Morus nigra), 37°11′10.8″ N / 3°41′21.2″ W*, 2016, watercolour on paper.

Trisha Hardwick, *Mulberries and Cream*, 2013, oils on linen.

work includes small constructions, like the wire cots in *Beds/Nature Series No. 10* (1993) and found objects, such as a lattice casement in *Windows* (2012), where silkworms have spun their cocoons. As part of the installation of this work, visitors can listen to the sound of silkworms munching on mulberry leaves.

English artist Jess Shepherd describes herself as a 'botanical painter'. Having trained first in botany, she brings a scientific precision to her work, which reaches an extraordinary level of detail in her *Leafscape* series of watercolour paintings of leaves. She explains that, even before her brush touches the paper, she tries to immerse herself in her subject, using all of her senses: 'One has to be aware of all these (sensory) elements in order to portray the plant well,' she says.[18] British artist Trisha Hardwick, however, draws her inspiration from the Spanish, Italian and Flemish still-life masters of the sixteenth–eighteenth centuries. She tries to use traditional, time-worn methods as far as possible, sourcing carefully milled paint to obtain bespoke colours. The work is mostly painted on fine-weave linen canvases.

Xanthe Mosley, *Veteran Morus nigra*, 2018, pencil on paper.

The inspiration to include mulberries in two of her paintings, she says, came from Stephen J. Bowe, author of a book on the material culture of the mulberry.[19]

British artist Xanthe Mosley has included several pencil drawings of mulberry trees in her *Drawing a Day* series – a commitment to post a drawing every day on Instagram. As some of the old mulberry trees – nearly all black mulberries – are in confined urban spaces, Mosley has an advantage over photographers in that she can choose to isolate the tree from a busy background, while being free of the optical constraints of a lens and camera that could otherwise introduce distortion or force the artist to crop the tree.

Mulberries in the Landscape

Unlike the mulberry in Ovid's *Metamorphoses*, the tree and its fruit do not occupy a central place in more recent literature. Rather, they often simply help set the scene as a defining part of the landscape, or as minor characters supporting the silkworm and silk rearing.

In his novel *The Fortune of the Rougons*, first published in 1871, Émile Zola uses mulberry trees to help paint a portrait of the landscape of the fictitious setting of Plassans in Provence (probably modelled on Aix-en-Provence). But one particular old tree plays a special and poignant role. This was to be the first in his monumental twenty-volume *Rougon-Macquart* series, which set out to present a 'natural and social history of a family under the Second Empire'. In the 1800s the Provençal landscape would have been populated with white mulberry trees planted for sericulture, supplying local *magnaneries*, whose cocoons and reeled silk would go off to weavers in Avignon and Lyons.

In a scene reminiscent of the opening scenes of *Pyramus and Thisbe*, two sweethearts, Silvère and Miette, whose lives are an intertwined thread though the novel, arrange to meet on the eve of Silvère's

Mulberry trees by the roadside in Gémenos, southern France, in the early 20th century.

Pruning mulberries by the roadside, photographer unknown.

departure to fight Napoleon's army, at the rectangular-shaped Aire Saint-Mittre:

> A narrow blind alley fringed with a row of hovels borders it on the right; while on the left, and at the further end, it is closed in by bits of wall overgrown with moss, above which can be seen the top branches of the mulberry-trees of the Jas-Meiffren – an extensive property with an entrance lower down the road. Enclosed upon three sides, the Aire

Saint-Mittre leads nowhere, and is only crossed by people out for a stroll.[20]

Silvère is waiting, playing with his vintage rifle and becoming impatient:

> When the young man had concealed his gun he again listened attentively, and still hearing nothing, resolved to climb upon the stone. The wall being low, he was able to rest his elbows on the coping. He could, however, perceive nothing except a flood of light beyond the row of mulberry-trees skirting the wall.
>
> Before he could stretch out his arms, however, a girl's head appeared above the wall. With singular agility the damsel had availed herself of the trunk of a mulberry-tree, and climbed aloft like a kitten. The ease and certainty with which she moved showed that she was familiar with this strange spot. In another moment she was seated on the coping of the wall. Then Silvère, taking her in his arms, carried her, though not without a struggle, to the seat.

The mulberry marked their meeting place and was to feature poignantly again at the end of the novel.

During the 'mulberry mania' years in France, Italy and Spain in the late seventeenth and nineteenth centuries, mulberry trees were often planted along roadsides and in hedgerows. Sericulture was a cottage industry performed by peasant farmers, so plantations of more than a terrace of mulberries have always been rare. In Italy the courtyard of a small farmer's house would often have a single, large mulberry tree, which furnished enough leaves to feed the hatchlings of 1 ounce (28 g) of silkworm eggs ('seeds').[21]

Sometimes, mulberry trees would be planted in the grounds around a manor house, and even used as part of its landscaping. This was the case in the Jas-Meiffren house in Zola's novel, at the end of the Faubourg: 'There stands the entrance to the Jas-Meiffren, an iron gate fixed to two strong pillars; a low row of mulberry-trees being visible through the bars. Silvère and Miette instinctively cast a glance inside as they passed on.'

Sericulture was clearly one of the occupations in the town, and was the responsibility of women and girls, like Miette, who was already working at the age of nine:

> The work of the peasant-woman in the South of France is much lighter than in the North. One seldom sees them employed in digging the ground, carrying loads, or doing other kinds of men's work. They bind sheaves, gather olives and mulberry leaves; perhaps their most laborious work is that of weeding. Miette worked away willingly. Open-air life was her delight, her health. So long as her aunt lived she was always smiling.

Zola also describes ancient mulberry trees in a later novel in the series, *Dr Pascal*. Here, the reference to terraces clearly refers to trees grown to feed silkworms: 'In the sunshine, the house, with its pink tiles, its walls distempered a bright yellow, looked wonderfully gay and attractive. Under the ancient mulberry trees on the terrace she revelled in their delightful coolness and admired the view.'[22] In the nineteenth century, when Zola was writing, old mulberry trees would have been a familiar sight in the countryside of the Midi.

Metaphor for a Lost Way of Life

Lebanese writer Iman Humaydan Younes, in her 2008 novel *Wild Mulberries*, is one of the rare authors to use the mulberry as a trope, rather than the silkworm. Set in a village in the mountains of Lebanon in the 1930s, the novel charts the decline of traditional local silk production, as the global market shifts. Despite a diminishing market for his home-produced silk, the Shaykh (head of the family) decides to expand his mulberry plantation from the terraces immediately surrounding the *haara* (traditional house) into the valley below. This requires even more manpower, just when the local labour force is abandoning the village for better employment prospects on the coast. The Shaykh's sister protests: 'people are uprooting mulberry trees to plant grapes and olive trees instead. The price of silk has gone to dirt and you're still growing mulberries.'[23]

When the Shaykh's son, Ibrahim, finally becomes disaffected with the whole enterprise and leaves home, too, the neglected terraces of mulberries gradually return to their wild state. This symbolizes the decline of an old way of life in a modernizing Lebanon, while the world stands unwittingly on the verge of a looming war. The book offers an insider account of the minutiae of rearing silkworms in a traditional small-scale rural enterprise and the central role played by the cultivation and harvesting of mulberry leaves, in what was once one of the leading countries for silk production in the Middle East.

Mulberries as Bit-players

One might expect the mulberry to play at least a supporting role in the short novel *Silk*, by Italian writer Alessandro Baricco, which became a bestseller in Italy (and a film in 2007). But he only mentions mulberries twice, and even then fleetingly. Set in the imaginary town of Lavilledieu, near Nîmes, in the 1860s, when domestic silkworms are decimated by the *pébrine* epidemic, the story tells of a trader in silkworm eggs who is forced to travel overland first to Persia, then on an epic journey to Japan once a year to source his supply.[24]

Virginia Woolf also uses silk and silkworms in her novel *Night and Day*, published in 1919, to help paint a portrait of Cassandra, the disappointing daughter of Lady Ottway, whose marriage prospects are looking slim:

> If the boys were clever, they won scholarships, and went to school; if they were not clever, they took what the family

Tins of *Bombyx mori* eggs ('seeds' or 'graines') from 1880.

connection had to offer them. The girls accepted situations occasionally, but there were always one or two at home, nursing sick animals, tending silkworms, or playing the flute in their bedrooms.

Lady Ottway was particularly peeved when, 'one day, she opened Cassandra's bedroom door on a mission of discovery, and found the ceiling hung with mulberry-leaves, the windows blocked with cages, and the tables stacked with home-made machines for the manufacture of silk dresses.' The prospect of making a silk dress from the few cocoons Cassandra may have been able to gather is clearly preposterous, while Woolf glosses over the daily headache of finding and gathering enough mulberry leaves to feed the silkworms.

In her autobiography *So Spins the Silkworm*, Zoe Lady Hart Dyke devotes several pages to her constant quest as a teenager to find fresh mulberry leaves to feed the clandestine silkworms in her bedroom at a finishing school in Tours, France. This involved nocturnal escapes out of an upstairs window and trips into town on her bicycle, as well as secret deliveries of leaves by local boys from the town. Fortunately for her, Tours, being a major centre for sericulture in the time of

Henri IV, was endowed with white mulberry trees. Zoe Lady Hart Dyke went on to start and run England's only successful silk farm, at Lullingstone, supplying parachutes to the troops in the Second World War.

More recently, Elise Valmorbida also uses the picking and shredding of mulberry leaves for silkworms to evoke life in rural northern Italy during and just after the fascist era in Italy, in her novel *The Madonna of the Mountains*.[25] According to the author, as part of her research she made frequent visits to two old black mulberry trees in the grounds of Dulwich Picture Gallery in south London.[26]

Metamorphosis

In his Pulitzer Prize-winning novel *Middlesex*, Jeffrey Eugenides uses the development and metamorphosis of the silkworm as an analogue to the unexpected gender change in store for Calliope Stephanides, the hermaphrodite heroine/hero of the story.[27] The story moves backwards and forwards in time and place, encompassing a silk-producing village on the slopes of Mount Olympia (high above Bursa in Turkey) in the 1920s; through Detroit during the Depression; ending in San Francisco in 1971.

Silk moth eggs, silkworms and silk cocoons pervade the story, holding together the various metamorphoses of the plot. But mulberries barely get a look in, even though the mulberry might have been a better trope for Caliope's hermaphroditic change from growing up as a girl to becoming a boy in her teens. Several mulberry species are monoecious (have both male and female flowers on the same tree) and individual trees can even change from being purely male to purely female in the course of their lifetimes.[28]

Mulberries in Folklore

Trees have been objects of worship since ancient times, particularly those that live for hundreds, if not thousands of years, such as the

Cristoforo de Predis(?), miniature from *Spherae coelestis et planetarum descriptio* (A Description of the Celestial Sphere and the Planets, 1470).

oak, yew and olive. The Romans considered the mulberry (along with the olive and the alder) sacred to Minerva, goddess of wisdom. In Sicily some people still maintain an ancient tradition of celebrating the Feast of St Nicolas on 6 December by cutting a mulberry branch and keeping it at home for a year. On a darker note, according to one German legend the Devil uses the roots of the mulberry tree to polish his boots, and so it has become a harbinger of evil.[29]

In English-speaking cultures, mulberries are probably best known from the rhyming ring-dance 'Here we go round the mulberry bush'. Most adults and children will be able to sing the first few lines, or possibly all of the verses, even if they have never seen a mulberry, or know that it is a tree and not a bush.

According to the nineteenth-century collector of folk tales and nursery rhymes James Orchard Halliwell, 'Here we go round the mulberry bush' is an example of 'a ring-dance imitation-play, the metrical portion of which is not without a little melody'.[30] Halliwell suggests, however, the rhyme was originally centred on the bramble or blackberry bush, and may have only switched to mulberry because the alliterative 'bramble bush' was not easy to sing. In this kind of

Walter Crane, illustration in *The Baby's Opera* (1877). The bush in the nursery rhyme 'Here we go round the mulberry bush' was probably originally a blackberry or bramble bush, not mulberry.

Rene Cloke, postcard by Valentine Ltd., 1939.

The mulberry has inspired myths and folk traditions since ancient times. Victorian decorative tiles, Belgrave Children's Hospital, produced in commemoration of the 150th anniversary of King's College Hospital in 1990.

ring-dance, all the children hold hands around an imaginary bush – which may also be represented by a child – and dance in a circle, singing:

> Here we go round the mulberry-bush,
> The mulberry-bush, the mulberry-bush:
> Here we go round the mulberry-bush
> On a cold and frosty morning!

The next verse starts with 'This is the way we wash our clothes'. As Halliwell explains,

> [the children] then dance round, repeating the first stanza, after which the operation of drying the clothes is commenced with a similar verse, 'This is the way we dry our clothes,' etc. The game may be continued almost *ad infinitum* by increasing the number of duties to be performed. They are, however,

generally satisfied with mangling, smoothing or ironing, the clothes, and then putting them away.[31]

Perhaps because of this association with childhood, mulberry trees have often been planted in school playgrounds, at least since the mid-nineteenth century, and some Victorian plantings survive today – sometimes even after the school has been demolished. For example, a mature black mulberry now stands, orphaned, on the corner of a 2007 housing estate in Lewisham (southeast London) on the site of the playground of a nineteenth-century boys' primary school, knocked down in the 1960s, but sparing the tree. Camden School for Girls in London also has a celebrated mulberry, and one school in east London was even known as the Mulberry School, with an image of the tree as its badge.

Although similar ring-dance rhymes, based on other bushes, have been recorded elsewhere, such as in Scandinavia, there are claims that the 'mulberry bush' rhyme originated in Wakefield Prison, in Yorkshire, which was once a workhouse for women. There is an old mulberry tree in the exercise yard today and the claim is that the women would have walked around it, singing the rhyme. But apart from the existence of the tree, which is probably 150 years old, there is no other evidence to support the story.

In the final chapter, we will look at some of the many uses to which the mulberry tree can be put.

six
Tree of Plenty

In India the mulberry is one of several trees known as *kalpavriksha* – tree of plenty. This is also the name given to a very real, ancient mulberry tree in Joshimath in Uttarakhand, where the ninth-century reformer of Hinduism Adiguru Shankaracharya is said to have meditated.

The term *kalpavriksha* is associated with the many uses to which all parts of the tree are put in India. The fruit provides jams and juice, the leaves are used for rearing silkworms and as fodder for cows and goats; the wood is used as fuel, for house construction, furniture making, and to make poles, toys and tea chests.

Some of the most ancient uses of the mulberry, besides its role in the organic alchemy of silk making, include textiles, paper and medicinal remedies.

Textiles

Mulberry-bark clothing was common in ancient China, alongside fabrics made from hemp. This turned out to be a first iteration of the use of mulberry derivatives for clothing, giving way to the exquisite, light, lustrous thread that silkworms spin naturally from the leaves of the same tree.

While all forms of mulberry taxa can be, and have been, used to make bark-cloth, the paper mulberry (*Broussonetia papyrifera*) came to be used extensively throughout East and Southeast Asia and into

Ancient Himalayan mulberry (*Morus serrata*) in Himachal Pradesh, India, which may be over 1,000 years old.

Oceania, following migrations from Taiwan and southeast China. The Maisin people of Papua New Guinea, for example, make their traditional tapa paper-like cloth from mulberry bark. Similar tapa cloth, under a variety of names, has been found in Samoa, Fiji and Hawaii and has even been used recently as an indicator for charting the migrations of people throughout Oceania.[1]

The Choctaw, Natchez and other Native American peoples use a very similar technique to make textiles from the inner bark of young branches from the endemic red mulberry (*Morus rubra*). In 1682 the explorers Henri de Tonti and Sieur de La Salle found sixty old men in a Natchez village (Taencas), sitting dressed in white cloaks that had been made by women from the inner bark of the red mulberry.[2]

Paper, Kites . . . and Money

Although writing may have originated in Mesopotamia around 3000 BCE, the first use of paper dates from the second century BCE in China. Up until then – and for centuries afterwards – written documents and drawings outside of China were made on clay, papyrus or parchment. Within China, silk was also used, but was expensive and impractical. The invention of paper, however, is usually attributed to Cai Lun – a eunuch government official in the service of Emperor He of the Han dynasty, in about 105 CE. Although he didn't actually invent paper, Cai Lun greatly improved its quality by mixing the mashed bark fibre pulp with hemp, rags and even fishing nets. Cai Lun seems to have based his idea for paper on the widespread use of bark fibres for textiles, often from the mulberry tree.

One of the earliest references to paper-making using the bark of the paper mulberry is found in a sixth-century text by Jia Sixie, a magistrate of Gaoyang district in modern Shandong province. He gives advice on cultivating the paper mulberry commercially, and mentions peeling and boiling the bark for paper as 'laborious but profitable'.[3]

According to Tsien Tsuen-Hsuin, in his volume on paper and printing for Joseph Needham's classic *Science and Civilisation in China*, 'Of all the products from the ancient world, few can compare in

Tapa cloth (*Siapo mamanu*) made from the bark of the paper mulberry. *c.* 1890.

significance with the Chinese inventions of paper and printing.'[4] James Millward, in his book *The Silk Road*, goes even further, arguing that the invention of paper — and its travel throughout the network of routes that came to be known as the Silk Road — may have had more impact on civilizations worldwide than silk.[5] While this may be true — especially after the invention of the printing press — paper-making, unlike sericulture, did not demand the presence of mulberry trees or lead to the obligatory, massive migration of specific tree species. The actual wood fibres used for the pulp varied according to the species of tree available locally.

Among the earliest users of mulberry paper for printing were Buddhist monks. The oldest known woodblock print — of a Buddhist scripture (the Great Dharani Sutra of Undefiled Pure Radiance) — was made on mulberry paper in around 706 CE, by monks in what is now Korea. It was discovered in the Sakyamuni Pagoda of Bulguksa Temple in Kyongju, Korea, in 1966.[6] Before this discovery, the oldest

Preparing cloth (tapa) from paper mulberry bark. Maui Nui Botanical Gardens, Maui, Hawaii, 2006.

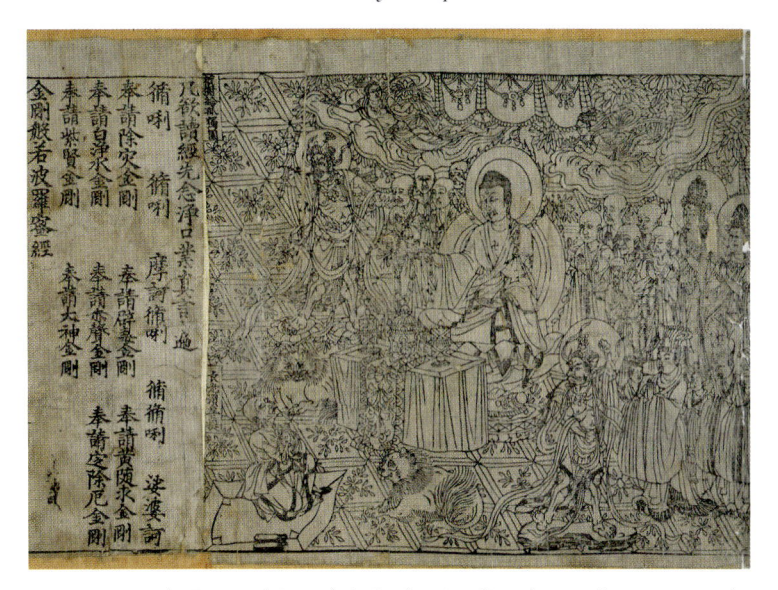

Frontispiece to the Diamond Sutra (c. 868 CE), printed in ink on mulberry paper in the 9th year of the Xiantong Era of the Tang Dynasty. Found in Cave 17, Dunhuang, by Sir Marc Aurel Stein in 1907.

dated woodblock print (on mulberry paper) had been a copy of the Diamond Sutra, discovered by a Daoist monk, Wang Yuanlu, in a cave library in Dunhuang, China, and dated to 868 CE. It was purchased by the Hungarian-born archaeologist Sir Marc Aurel Stein at the site in 1907 and is still the oldest complete example of a printed book. It is made of seven strips of yellow paper, pasted together in a scroll, 5 metres (16 ft) long.

Soon after the techniques of paper-making had spread throughout China, it was used to make objects, such as kites, which had previously been made of silk. In recent times (1951), the Japanese sculptor Isamu Noguchi designed his famous bamboo and mulberry paper lamps, copies of which are sold in home furnishing shops all over the world. Mulberry paper has also long been used, especially in Japan and Korea, for windows and screens, instead of glass.

Korea and Japan had also learned the Chinese techniques of paper-making by the sixth century CE, using similar materials to the Chinese. Traditional Korean *hanji* paper is made from the bark of the paper mulberry (known as *Dak*), which, after being boiled, pounded and dried, is coated with sap from the Aibika plant (*Abelmoschus manihot*), a member of the mallow family and similar to hibiscus. During the Goryeo kingdom (918–1392 CE), *hanji* reached a peak of renown throughout the region, with ground gold and silver pigments typically applied to indigo-dyed paper. *Hanji* was traded for precious items, including pearls.

As the technique of paper-making spread throughout Arab countries and beyond, it was adapted to local raw materials and also to cultural factors. In Arab (and Western) countries, where a quill was used for writing, a smooth coating was needed, while in China, Japan and Korea, where a brush was used, the surface could be rougher. Much the same artisanal techniques of paper-making used along the Silk Road in the Middle Ages can still be observed in countries such as Uzbekistan today.[7]

Paper Money

Another revolutionary Chinese invention using mulberry bark was paper money, famously recorded by the Venetian merchant Marco Polo in the thirteenth century, on his travels to visit Kublai Khan during the Yuan dynasty (1271–1368 CE). As Marco Polo observed:

> the emperor's mint is in this city of Khanbaliq . . . he has money made for him in the following way. He has the bark stripped from trees – to be precise, from the mulberry trees whose leaves are eaten by silkworms. Then the thin layer of bast between the bark and the wood of the tree is removed. After being ground and pounded it is pressed with the aid of glue into sheets like those of cotton paper, which are completely black. And when these sheets are ready they are cut up into pieces of different sizes, rectangular in shape and of greater length than breadth.[8]

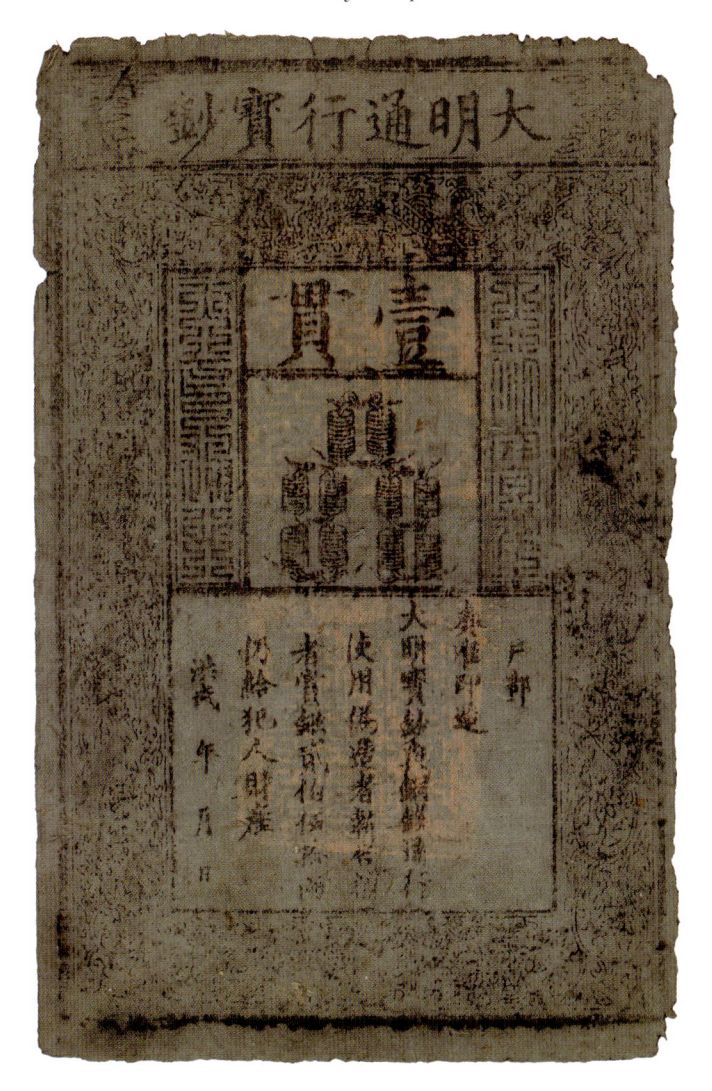

Ming dynasty 1 guan (1 string of 1,000 coins) mulberry paper banknote, from Hongwu, China, 1375.

These notes were then sealed, signed and stamped, becoming money 'with as much authority and solemnity as if they were cast from pure gold or silver', with the 'ultimate penalty' for anyone who dared forge them.[9] A tenth-century CE text by Su Yijian confirms that mulberry bark (*sang-pi*) was used in the north of China for

Black mulberries stain everything.

paper, and not the paper mulberry (*Broussonetia papyrifera*), which is not a *Morus* species.[10]

The earliest paper money is, in fact, much older, dating back to the Tang dynasty (618–907 CE), but no examples have survived. A few paper notes from the Ming dynasty, modelled on the Yuan dynasty notes, are in collections at the British Museum and the British Library. As Caroline Cartwright and her colleagues at the British Museum and British Library have pointed out, the exact composition of the notes has intrigued scholars, as the description 'mulberry paper' is unacceptably vague:

> The dark colours and limp appearance of the notes seen today have been attributed to the processing of fibres from mulberry bark, but it was not clear which kind of mulberry:

Morus alba (white mulberry); *Morus australis*, formerly known as *Morus bombycis* (Chinese mulberry); *Broussonetia papyrifera* (paper mulberry); or *Broussonetia kazinoki* (Japanese paper mulberry or *chu*).[11]

So, the authors decided to carry out scanning electronic microscope analysis of the fibres in the notes. The results of the examination were rather surprising:

> while white mulberry and paper mulberry had been used in the manufacture of the Ming notes in the British Museum and British Library collections, many other raw material sources had also been exploited, such as bamboo, rice straw, wheat straw, hibiscus and hemp. As these notes were hitherto believed to be made from mulberry bark (taxon unspecified), these results have important implications and provide a reference point for ongoing research by specialist scholars from which new and challenging avenues of interest are expected to emerge.[12]

Dyes

Anyone who has picked black mulberry fruit will know how readily it stains – hands, clothes, pavements and just about anything else. This has not been lost on craftspeople wherever the mulberry grows, be it endemic or introduced. The one-hundred-year-old Pennsylvania-based crayon company, Crayola included 'mulberry' – the distinctive dark red of the black mulberry fruit – as one of its colour range from 1958 until it was finally 'retired' in 2003. The Old English term 'murrey' derives from the colour of the black mulberry and was used in the livery colours of the House of York in the fifteenth century. In Thomas Hardy's novel *Jude the Obscure*, published in 1895, Sue Brideshead 'wore a murrey coloured dress with a little lace collar' when she met Jude at Melchester.[13]

The Native American Timucua of northeast Florida used the leaves, twigs and berries of the red mulberry to make dyes, while the Internet abounds with modern-day recipes for natural dyes using mulberry fruit, from France and Australia to Laos and Thailand. The Plants for a Future (PFAF) database cites a brown dye as being derived from the trunk of the white mulberry.[14] A red-violet to dark-purple dye is obtained from the fruit of the black mulberry and a yellow-green dye is obtained from the leaves. Chemical analyses have isolated the flavonols, morin and rutin as the active agents in mulberry dyes, as well as the flavone, mulberrin, present in the wood, which creates golden and yellow colours.[15]

The blood-red juice has even been used to frighten the enemy in battle. According to the apocryphal book of the Bible 1 Maccabees 6, the boy ruler of the Seleucid Syrian empire, Antiochus V Eupator, and his protector, Lysias, besieged Beth-Zur (29 kilometres, or 18 mi., from Jerusalem, in the mountains of Hebron). Judas Maccabee raised an army against them and pitched camp at nearby Bath-Zacharias, south of Bethlehem. Anthiochus and Lysias went to fight Judas, with a massive army of 100,000 men, 20,000 horses and 32 elephants:

> The king rising very early marched fiercely with his host toward Bath-Zacharias, where his armies made them ready to battle, and sounded the trumpets.
> And to the end they might provoke the elephants to fight, they shewed them the blood of grapes and mulberries.
> (1 Maccabees 6)

When Judas's younger brother, Eleazor Horan, was crushed by the elephant that he had run through with a sword in a last-ditch rallying display of courage, the Maccabean army withdrew, only to win another day.

Some scholars have taken the biblical description literally, assuming that the sight of what appeared to be blood (mulberry and grape juice, for example) excited the elephants to fight. Others think that 'shewed' is a mistranslation of the Hebrew and that, in fact, the elephants were given a wine made of fermented grapes and mulberries. They would therefore have been drunk when they went into battle and likely to be erratically dangerous.

The nineteenth-century natural philosopher Victor Hehn describes a more benign use for the staining properties of mulberries: 'Luxurious ladies, and gay people who went masquerading painted their temples and cheeks with the juice of mulberries; and the wine they drank, when too pale, was very likely also darkened with the red juice, as is even now the custom in the South.'[16] Incidentally, for those bent on foraging for ripe black mulberries in summer, a good way to remove the purple stains from skin and clothes is to rub them with a crushed, unripe mulberry (or mulberry leaf).

Food and Nutrition

The fruit of the black mulberry is generally prized for its juicy, tart sweetness, whether grown in its native Central Asia or the Middle East, or in far-off countries where it has been introduced. As the fruit is only ripe for a month or so in summer (and then in almost excessive abundance), its appearance traditionally triggers a flurry of harvesting activity. From Iran to Azerbaijan, children scramble up the trunk and shake the branches, causing the ripe fruit to drop onto a net or blanket that has been spread on the ground under the canopy.

Even in London, mature and publicly accessible black mulberry trees can become closely guarded secrets in some ethnic communities that use the fruit in their traditional cooking. So, local Turkish residents climb an old mulberry in a stately home in Enfield (north London), while local Nepalese families forage the four-hundred-year-old tree of its fruit at Charlton House (southeast London), often before the chef can get hold of them for her home-made pies. Black mulberries, too, originally from a tree in the Friends' burial ground in Tottenham (north London), provide the pink colouring for the icing in a traditional sponge called 'Tottenham cake'.

We know that the Romans ate black mulberries at their feasts. The Roman poet Horace (65–68 BCE) recommends picking them in the morning, as we have already seen:

> I'll give him Health, who when his Meals are done
> Eats juicy *Mulberries*, pluck'd before the Sun
> Doth rise too high, and scorch with heat of the Noon.[17]

The Romans introduced the black mulberry as they gradually conquered Europe. It was mainly grown for its fruit and seems to have remained a tree associated with the well-off, living in urban areas (and not the military as has often been suggested).[18]

The Calendar of Córdoba (*Kitāb fī tafṣīl al-zamān wa-maṣāliṣ al-abdān*), a medieval Andalusian text, completed in 961 CE, offered practical advice on growing fruit and vegetables in the walled garden of an Islamic villa (*munya*) in Iberia at the time. The black mulberry (*firsad*) is mentioned, and the fruit was used to make a sweet syrup.[19] In England, at about the same time, the Anglo-Saxons made a kind of mead wine called *Morat* from honey and mulberry juice – although herbalist and plantswoman Maud Grieve thinks the *Morum* referred to may have been the blackberry.[20] The seventeenth-century diarist John Evelyn seems to have known of this: 'As for drink, the juice of the berry mixed with cider-apples, makes an excellent liquor, both for colour and taste.'[21] Grieve, in her *A Modern Herbal*, also writes that: 'In the East the Mulberry is most productive and useful. It is gathered when ripe and dried on the tops of houses in the sun, and stored for winter use. In Cabul, it is pounded to a fine powder, and mixed with flour for bread.'[22] John Evelyn had a note of caution to add to this particular use, though: 'I have read, that in Syria they make bread of them [mulberries]; but that the eating of it makes men bald.'[23]

The fruit of the white mulberry is not so highly prized as that of the black. The seventeenth-century French specialist on silk and

Gathering mulberry fruit for dessert in Tajikistan, 2011.

mulberries Olivier de Serres wrote of the white mulberry that 'the fruit is disagreeable of taste, for his flashie sweetness, whereby it is not edible by others than by women which have lost their relish, children, and poore people in time of famine.'[24] However, some white mulberry varieties produce black fruits that are not excessively sweet or bland and also find their way into pies, sorbets and jams. The white mulberry has the advantage over the black that its ripe fruit can be dried and therefore preserved. Some are even coated in raw chocolate as an unusual sweet and sold in health food stores.

Native Americans ate the indigenous red mulberry, as the Spanish explorer Hernando de Soto noted in 1540, when he found dense

groves of cultivated mulberries in a Muskogee village in Georgia.[25] The Iroquois made cakes with the fruit and kept them to be eaten in the winter months, while the Cherokee mixed the berries with sugar and cornmeal to make dumplings.

The seventeenth-century philosopher and politician Francis Bacon seems to have been caught up with the fashion for mulberries in England at the time, and likely planted the tree in his home at Canonbury, London, that is still growing there today. Bacon observed that the mulberry, particularly *M. nigra*, was a good source of manna, reminiscent of the food that God provided to the Israelites during their forty-day travels in the desert:

> The manna of Calabria is the best, and in most plenty. They gather it from the leaf of the mulberry-tree; but not of such mulberry trees as grow in the vallies. And manna falleth upon the leaves by night, as other dews do. It should seem, that before those dews come upon trees in the vallies, they dissipate and cannot hold out. It should seem also, the mulberry-leaf itself hath some coagulating virtue, which inspissateth the dew, for that it is not found upon other trees: and we see by the silk-worm, which feedeth upon that leaf, what a dainty smooth juice it hath; and the leaves also, especially of the black mulberry, are somewhat bristly, which may help to preserve the dew. Certainly it were not amiss to observe a little better the dews that fall upon trees, or herbs growing on mountains; for it may be many dews fall, that spend before they come to the vallies. And I suppose, that he would gather the best May-dew for medicine, should gather it from the hills.[26]

The nutritional value of the mulberry has recently been emphasized by the United Nations Food and Agriculture Organization

Mulberry pattern textile by Moda Fabric.

(fao) in a concerted effort to promote the use of mulberry leaves and branches to feed pigs and cattle, especially in developing countries.[27] When the European sericulture boom of the nineteenth century peaked and crashed, this is precisely the use to which farmers put their mulberry trees – a practice maintained to this day in eastern Europe.

In Turkey, both black and white mulberries are used in recipes for sorbets, cakes, brownies and crumbles and boiled to make *Pekmez* – a kind of syrup that is mixed with tahini for breakfast or used as a treatment for anaemia.[28] The fruit does, indeed, contain significant amounts of iron. Interestingly, as we have seen, Turkish sericulture was hit in the nineteenth century by the combined blows of *pébrine* and the increasing availability of cheap Japanese silk, Turkey saw the crisis as an opportunity. While gradually abandoning sericulture, farmers did not grub out – or abandon – their mulberry trees, as the French had done. Rather, they saw an opening for a new lucrative fruit market.

White mulberries do not disintegrate when they are picked and so can be sold fresh on markets, or dried for domestic use or export. A major exporter of fruit, Turkey produces about 70,000 tonnes of white mulberries a year. Nowadays, most mulberry cultivation in Turkey – which is distributed around the country, although it was once focused on the port city of Bursa – is for fruit.

Medicine

It is well known that there are links between food, nutrition and medicine. In traditional Chinese medicine (tcm), for example, illness is seen in terms of imbalances – between hot and cold, yin and yang, masculine and feminine, hard and soft. Health is, conversely, maintained by ensuring balance – in what one eats, between body and mind, and so on. A healthy Chinese diet will thus aim to blend nutrients to maintain this balance, while tcm remedies will add or subtract nutrients to correct the imbalance. The almost ubiquitous mulberry plays an important role in tcm.

Just about all parts of the mulberry tree – leaves, fruit, bark and roots – have been used for millennia, in different parts of the world, to treat a diverse range of ailments, from toothache and snake-bites to sore throats and diabetes. In his 1599 georgic poem *The Silkwormes and their Flies*, Thomas Moffet summed up this extensive pharmacopoeia:

I leave to tell how she doth poison cure,
From adders goare or gall of Lisards got,
What burning blaines she heales and sores impure,
In palat, iawes, and al enflamed throte,
What canckars hard, and wolfes be at her lure,
What Gangrenes stoop that make our toes to rotte:
Briefly, few griefes from Panders boxe out-flew,
But here they finde a medcine, old or new.

Her bloud retourn'd to sweete Thisbean wine,
Strengthneth the lungs and stomacke ouer-weake,
Her clustred grapes do prove a dish most fine,
Whose kernels soft do stones in sunder breake:
Her leaves too that converted are in time,
Which kings themselves in highest prize do reake:
Thus gives she meat, and drink, medcine, & cloth,
To ev'ry one that is not drownd in sloth.

A recent summary of the pharmacological uses of the mulberry makes impressive reading. Different parts of *Morus alba* have been found to be useful in treating elephantiasis and tetanus. Extracts are analgesic, sedative, antibacterial, astringent, diaphoretic, hypoglycaemic, odontalgic, antirheumatic, diuretic and may have uses in the treatment of premature greying, tinnitus, incontinence, constipation, as well as being used to treat colds, influenza, eye infections, nosebleeds and toothache.[29] Extracts of the white mulberry are included in a modern hand lotion by Molton Brown, with allusions in its advertising to the misty mountains of the Cévennes in France where the trees still grow after the demise of the region's silk industry.

It is interesting to see how different societies have come to similar conclusions about the medicinal uses of parts of the mulberry, giving the claims an extra measure of credibility. Let's start at the top.

Eyes

In TCM, all parts of the mulberry are used to treat imbalances in the liver and hence the eyes, which are the 'window' to the liver. Nutritional analysis of mulberry fruit reveals that it is a good source of lutein and zeaxanthin, which are selectively absorbed by the retinal *macula lutea* (fovea) which is responsible for sharp central vision.

Mouth, Teeth and Throat

John Evelyn mentions the 'soveraign qualities' of mulberry fruit for 'relaxing of the belly, being eaten in the morning, and curing inflamations and ulcers of the mouth and throat, mix'd with *Mel rosarum*, in which receipt they do best, being taken before they are over-ripe'.[30]

In his *Natural History*, Pliny the Elder cites a similar benefit from mulberry root mixed with mashed earthworms and vinegar:

> Earthworms, boiled down in oil and poured into the ear on the side where there is pain, afford relief. These also, reduced

M. alba fruit and leaf on Ukraine postage stamp.

Birds love mulberry fruit. *M. alba* in Himachal Pradesh, India, 2016.

to ash and plugged into decayed teeth, force them to fall out easily, and applied to sound teeth relieve any pain in them. They should be burnt, however, in an earthen pot. They also benefit if boiled down in squill vinegar with the root of a mulberry tree, so as to make a wash for the teeth.[31]

Pliny refers several times to 'stomatice', by which he means remedies for mouth afflictions:

> There must also be given a recipe of the ancients. The juice of the ripe fruit was mixed with that of the unripe, and the two boiled in a copper vessel to the consistency of honey. Some used to add myrrh and cypress and then to bake the mixture very hard in the sun, stirring it three times a day with a spatula. This was their stomatice . . .

In the same section he also recommends that 'an incision into the root [of the mulberry] at the time of harvest yields a juice admirably suited to relieve toothache, gatherings and suppurations, besides acting as a purge.'[32] A version of this remedy seems to have passed to William Turner, the sixteenth-century English botanist, doctor, apothecary, dean of Wells cathedral and gardener to Lord Somerset at Syon House:

> It is good to wash the aching teeth with the broth of the bark and leaves hot, to drive the pain away. The roots being cut, nicked, or scotched, about the last end of the harvest, ye must make a furrow round about it, and it will put forth a juice which ye may find in the next day after clumpered or grown together. This juice is exceeding good for the toothache; it scattereth and driveth away swelling lumps and purgeth the belly.[33]

Pliny gives other remedies for the mouth and throat using mulberry fruit:

> There is made from the mulberry a mouthwash called *panchrestos*, or *arteriace*, in the following way. Three sextarii of the juice from the fruit are reduced by a gentle heat to the consistency of honey; then are added two denarii of dried omphacium, or one of myrrh, and one denarius of saffron. These are beaten up together and mixed with the decoction. There is no other remedy more pleasant for the mouth, the

trachea, the uvula or the gullet. It is also prepared in another way. Two sextarii of the juice and one sextarius of Attic honey are boiled down in the manner I have described above.[34]

Interestingly, a twentieth-century guide to the medicinal value of plants growing in Greece still recommends using the fresh fruit or making a mulberry honey to treat mouth ulcers and irritation of the mucous membranes in the mouth.[35]

Stomach and Intestines

For William Turner, this time quoting from the tenth-century Persian polymath Avicenna (or Ibn Sina): 'the leaves of the mulberry are a sovereign remedy for the squinscy or sqinancy and against strangling'. He adds, this time passing on a remedy handed down from Galen, a Greek physician in the Roman Empire (second–third century CE), in his *De facultatibus alimenentorum*:

> the rype fruit of the mulberry doutles softeneth the belly. But the unripe fruit after that it is dryed is a very bynding medicine wherefore it is good for the blody flix [that is, dysentery] or for any other flix. But it must be brayed & cast into your meat as ye do with somach: or if a man will he may drynk it with wyne & water.[36]

John Evelyn agreed that the mulberry was useful for 'relaxing the belly', while Pliny wrote that juice squeezed from dried mulberry fruit 'was useful whenever astringent treatment of the bowels was called for'.[37]

Various Native Americans, including the Comanche, used the indigenous red mulberry to treat dysentery and as a diuretic. The Cherokee steeped mulberry bark and drank the liquid to loosen the stool and get rid of intestinal worms. William Turner was also aware (via Galen) that 'in the bark of the root the purging virtue excelleth with a certain bitterness, in so much that it can kill a broad worm.'[38]

While on the subject of worms – although an affliction of the skin, not the gut – the Rappahannock Native Americans rubbed sap from the red mulberry over the skin to treat ringworm, a practice also known to the Cherokee and Comanche.

Blood

There are several references in herbals and medical treatises to the use of parts of the mulberry in stemming the flow of blood (presumably therefore as a coagulant). Often, particularly when used to treat heavy menstrual periods, there is an added element of magic or superstition involved. So, we find Pliny saying:

> When it begins to bud, but before the leaves unfold, the fruit-to-be is plucked with the left hand. The Greeks call them *ricini*. These, if they have not touched the ground, when worn as an amulet stay a flow of blood, whether it flows from a wound, the mouth, the nostrils, or from haemorrhoids. For this purpose they are stored away and kept.
>
> The same effect is said to be produced if there be broken off at a full moon a branch beginning to bear; it must not touch the ground, and is specially useful when tied on the upper arm of a woman to prevent excessive menstruation. It is thought that the same result is obtained if the woman herself breaks off a branch at any time, provided that it does not touch the ground before it is used as an amulet.[39]

A more convoluted version of this is found in the tenth-century *Medicina de quadrupedibus*, written in Middle English:

> Against flux of blood, when to all men the moon is seventeen nights old, after the setting of the sun, come then to the tree which is called mulberry tree and take from it an apple [berry] with thy left hand with two fingers, that is with

Black mulberry with ripe and unripe fruit in Allen Hall seminary, Chelsea, London, on the site of Thomas More's house.

the thumb and the ring finger, a white apple, which as yet is not ruddy; then lift it up and up arise: this is useful for the upper part of the body. Again put it down and lout down [bow down] over it: it is profitable for the lower part of the body. Before then thou take this apple, say then these words: 'I take thee' etc. When thou hast said these words, take the apple and wind it up in a fine purple cloth, and see that this leechdom [remedy] touch neither water nor earth. When there is need, and the upper part of the body labours in any sore, or any difficulties, bind [it] upon the forehead; if it is on the lower part, bind [it] on the womb.

Ad mulieris fluxum [or, for menstrual bleeding,] let her take the comb with which she alone combs her head (hair), with which no other person combed it before nor ever shall comb it after. But under the mulberry-tree there let her comb her hair, let her gather what is lost in the comb and hang it on an upstanding twig of the mulberry-tree, and again after a while, when clean, let her gather it [from the twig] and preserve it: that shall be a leechdom for her, for the one who there combs her head. If thou wish a woman to be cleansed who never might be cleansed, work her a salve from the hair and dry it somewhat and put it on her body; then shall she be cleansed.[40]

In India, Ayurvedic medicine uses the native mulberry species, *Morus indica*, in remedies to reduce blood pressure and cholesterol. There seems to be a scientific basis for this. The United States Department of Agriculture (USDA) gives a detailed breakdown of the nutrient composition of a whole range of foods, including mulberries.[41] This has been usefully summarized and interpreted by nutritionist Umesh Rudrappa.[42]

Raw mulberry fruit contains good amounts of the minerals potassium, manganese and magnesium. Potassium helps control heart rate and blood pressure, while manganese is co-factor for the antioxidant enzyme superoxide dismutase. The berries also contain resveratrol, which is a polyphenol flavonoid antioxidant. This offers some protection against the risk of stroke by altering molecular mechanisms to reduce blood vessel constriction, while increasing the production of the vasodilator hormone, nitric oxide.

Particularly in *Morus* species that produce dark purple/red fruit, the juice contains high levels of iron, which is useful in combating anaemia. This is a well-known and popular remedy in countries where mulberries are abundant, such as Turkey (see above in this chapter).

Metabolic Disorders: Diabetes and Gout

The English botanist and herbalist John Gerard (1545–1612) wrote of the benefits of the mulberry in treating gout, by describing what happens if the fruit is not available:

> Hegelander in Athenaeus affirmeth, that the Mulberrie trees in his time did not bring forth fruit in twentie years together, and that so great a plague of the gout then raigned and raged so generally, as not onely men but boyes, wenches, eunuchs and women were troubled with that disease.[43]

But perhaps the most exciting and well-researched health benefits of the mulberry relate to its use in reducing blood sugar levels, and hence in treating Type 2 diabetes and some other metabolic disorders. In many ways this was an obvious potential therapeutic use, as it is precisely by interfering with pathways for absorbing sugars that mulberry sap kills off just about all insect predators except the larvae of the *Bombyx mori* silk-moth. Because this activity has been known for some time, there has been considerable research to isolate and test the bioactive components in various parts of different species of mulberry.[44]

Traditional Chinese medicine has long used infusions of dried *M. alba* leaves to treat Type 2 diabetes, whose symptoms of thirst and frequent urination characterize it as a pathology known as 'Yin deficiency and dry heat'. We now know that mulberry leaves contain a range of alkaloids, flavonoids, polysaccharides and amino acids with specific anti-diabetic (hypoglycemic) effects.[45]

Raw mulberry fruit also contain large amounts of a whole range of antioxidants, including vitamin C and other vitamins, which neutralize free radicals. These are highly reactive, rogue molecules that can create havoc in the body, and are thought to play a role in human diseases, including Type 2 diabetes, arthritis, heart disease and cancer.

Overleaf: The Wilkin & Son jam company in Tiptree, Essex, has the largest commercial mulberry orchard in the UK.

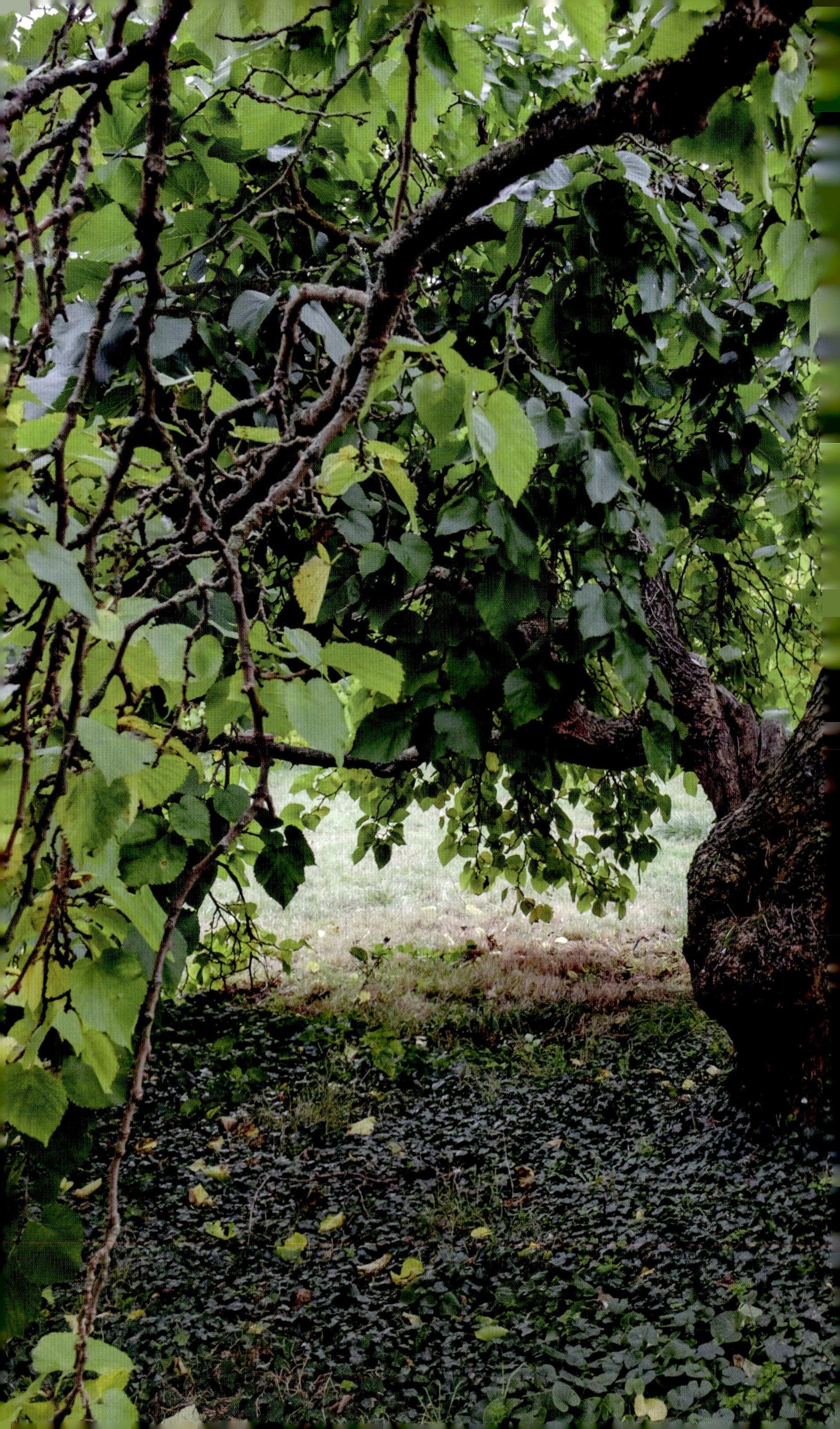

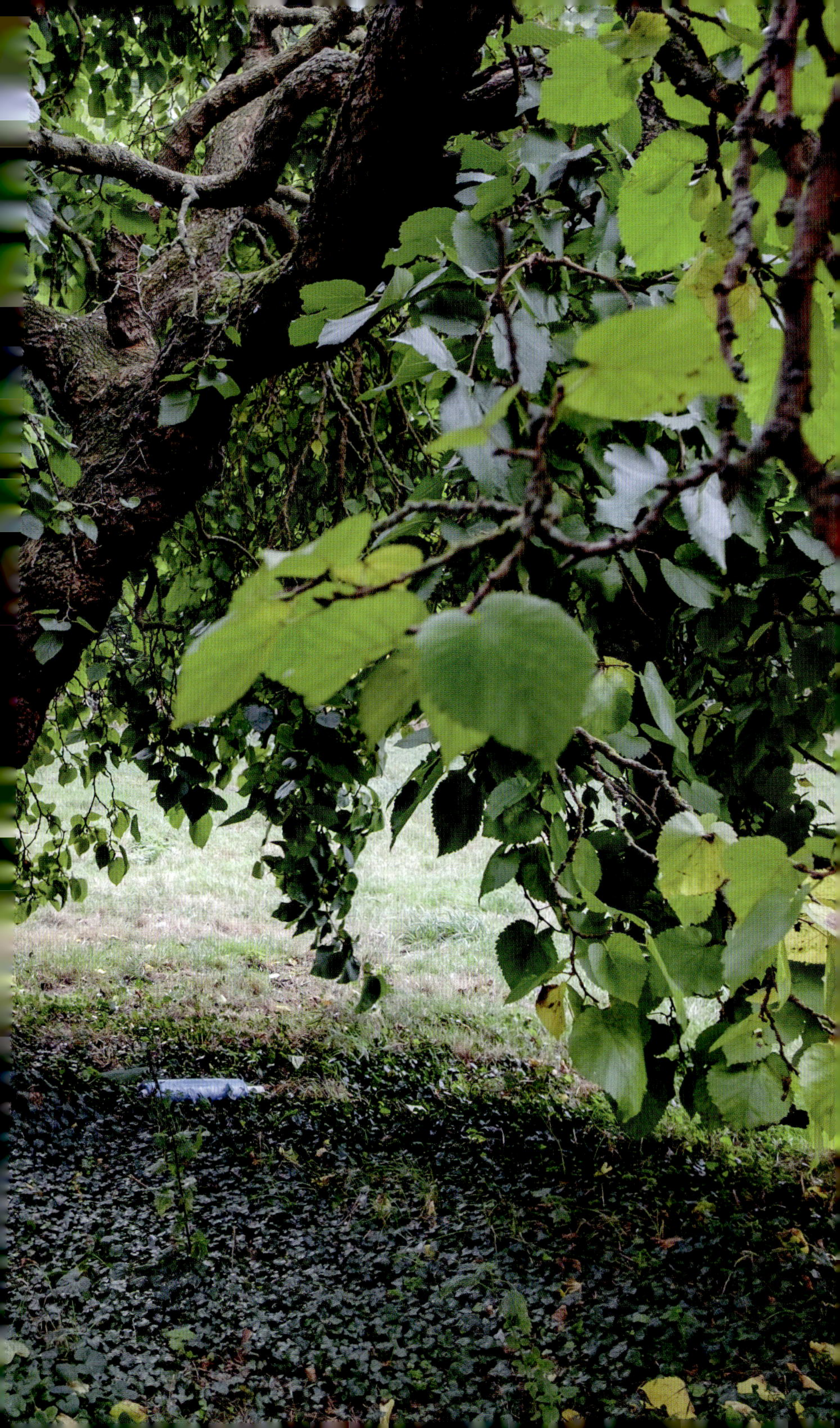

Antidote to Poisons

The mulberry's anti-venom and anti-toxin properties have often been vaunted. For Moffet, the mulberry 'doth poison cure/ From adders goare or gall of Lisards got'.[46] William Turner claimed that 'The bark is a treacle against the poison of henbayn.'[47] He also suggested that 'the juice of the leaves taken in the quantity of a cyst is a good remedy against the biting of the field spider.'[48] And, for Pliny the Elder:

> Mulberry leaves pounded, or a decoction of dried leaves, are used as an application for snake bite, and it is of some benefit to take them in drink. The juice extracted from the skin of the root, and drunk in wine or diluted vinegar, counteracts the poison of scorpions.[49]

Wood

Wherever the mulberry grows, people have found various uses for the timber. The Seminole, a Native American tribe who broke away from the Muscogee (Creeks) in the eighteenth century and settled in what is now Florida, used the branches of the red mulberry to make bows. The timber was also used for boats, tubs and small domestic objects. The American naturalist William Bartram, travelling through the Carolinas and Florida in the mid-eighteenth century, found red mulberries being cultivated in orchards in abandoned Native American villages.

Musical Instruments

As a hard wood, mulberry is used for the bodies of several stringed instruments (chordophones), from Japan to Central Asia and Greece. Its durability means it does not vibrate well and so is not usually used for the soundboards of these instruments, though. An exception is the Japanese *Satsuma biwa* lute, where all parts of the instrument are made from white mulberry. Unlike other mulberry-based lutes, however, which use highly resonating materials for the soundboard, the *biwa* is played by vigorous percussive striking with a wooden plectrum, rather than more gentle plucking.[50]

In Central Asia and Silk Road countries, mulberry wood (often *M. alba*) is used for the bodies of a number of lute-like stringed musical instruments, such as the Cretan *lyra*, the Turkish *saz*, the Iranian *setar* and the Greek *bouzouki*. But none is perhaps so renowned as the *tar*, a six-stringed instrument with a waisted body and long neck, which is found throughout Iran, Azerbaijan, Armenia, Georgia and in and around the Caucasus region. First appearing in Persia in the mid-eighteenth century, the body of the instrument is usually made from

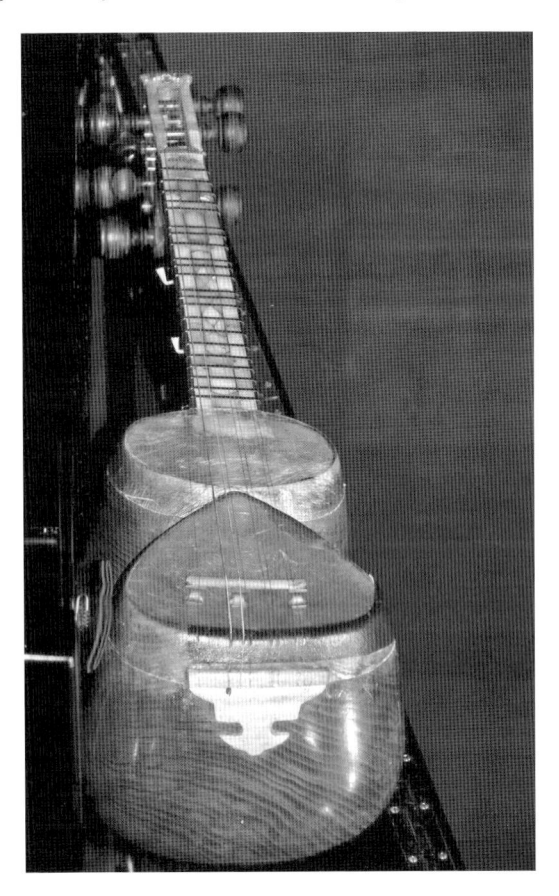

Azerbaijani *tar* made from mulberry wood.

a hollowed-out piece of mulberry wood – white or black – the older the better. The sounding board is traditionally made from the thin pericardium that envelops the heart of an ox or cow, and the neck from walnut.

The 'Craftsmanship and performance art of the Tar, a long-necked string musical instrument', was added to the UNESCO List of Intangible Cultural Heritage in 2012. With the six strings of the *tar* traditionally made of silk, the mulberry has acquired a sacred status in Azerbaijan. While some versions of the instrument can be quite plain, others are exquisitely inlaid with mother-of-pearl, ivory and

Magic lantern slide of a slice of black mulberry wood.

marquetry. The *balaban*, an oboe-like wind instrument made from mulberry wood is also found in Azerbaijan.

An even more ancient Central Asian lute made from mulberry is the Afghan *rubab*, which can trace its origins at least back to the seventh century CE. Traditionally the master luthier would undertake a whole series of ritual acts before and during the making of a new *rubab*. He would start with ablution and prayer, then the sacrifice of a sheep, which would be skinned and the meat cooked and shared. The sheep's gut would be reserved for the strings and the stretched skin used for the soundboard. A suitable piece of wood from an aged mulberry tree (or apricot) would be soaked in water for ten to fifteen days to prevent it from cracking. Mulberry *rubab*s can be found in Pamiri houses that are more than one hundred years old.[51]

In Turkey the *saz* – a stringed instrument made from mulberry, walnut, hornbeam or juniper (sometimes with alternating strips of two of these woods for decorative effect) – ranks in importance for a man alongside his wife, his horse and his weapon; it is a calamity if it should be destroyed.[52]

Furniture and Wooden Objects

When John Evelyn was writing *Sylva*, his classic *Discourse of Forest-trees and the Propagation of Timber* (1664), there were very few mulberry trees of any significant size or age in England, so mulberry timber gets a rather cursory mention. Most of his chapter on the mulberry is devoted to its cultivation to feed silkworms, extolling the virtues of *Morus alba*, the white mulberry, which is (and was then) almost totally absent in Britain. Nevertheless, he does say that the 'durableness' of (black) mulberry timber could be of 'incomparable benefit' for the joiner or carpenter 'and to make hoops, bows, wheels, and even ribs for small vessels, instead of oak &c.'[53]

Evelyn does not mention the traditional use of mulberry wood to make hockey sticks, though the game was probably being played at the time. The origin of the game is not known for certain, but a clue may lie in the possible derivation of 'hockey' from the French *hoquet*, meaning a shepherd's crook. Both sheep and mulberries are common in the Cévennes region of France.

Four centuries later, Peter Goodwin, the director of one of Britain's leading cabinetmaking companies, Titchmarsh & Goodwin, echoes this recommendation in his foreword to Stephen Bowe's informative and sumptuously illustrated book, *Mulberry*. The wood from the black mulberry, he says, has 'very desirable qualities, such as the complex grain patterns, high chance of burr configuration and a golden colour which gradually darkens with time'.[54] Some of the young mulberries of Evelyn's day have today matured into gnarled, collapsed veterans, but, says Goodwin, they are usually so venerated by their owners that the wood almost never comes into the hands of British furniture makers and craftspeople. This changed for a while, though, when the 1987 hurricane brought down several old mulberries, suddenly making the rare and sought-after timber available. Sometimes there is enough to make a tabletop or large piece of furniture, but more often the wood is used to make 'treen' (small, functional objects).

Shakespeare's Casket

A famous example of one of these objects is a casket made from the wood of a black mulberry that was growing at William Shakespeare's New Place home in Stratford-upon-Avon, around 1602. The casket, now in the British Museum, was presented to the great Shakespearean actor David Garrick in 1769, along with a scroll and a goblet, also made of wood from the Bard's mulberry when he was given the freedom of Stratford-upon-Avon. Garrick wrote a song for the presentation ceremony:

> Behold this fair goblet, 'twas carved from the tree,
> Which, O my sweet SHAKESPEARE, was planted by thee;
> As a relick I kiss it, and bow at the shrine,
> What comes from thy hand must be ever divine!

Followed by a chorus:

> All shall yield to the Mulberry tree,
> Bend to thee,
> Blest Mulberry,
> Matchless was he
> Who planted thee,
> And thou like him immortal be![55]

The poet William Cowper (1731–1800) also referred to Shakespeare's mulberry tree and Garrick's casket in his poem *The Task*:

> The mulberry-tree was hung with blooming wreaths,
> The mulberry-tree stood centre of the dance,
> The mulberry-tree was hymned with dulcet airs,
> And from his touchwood trunk the mulberry-tree
> Supplied such relics as devotion holds
> Still sacred, and preserves with pious care.[56]

How the wood to make Garrick's goblet and casket came to be available is a rather tragic tale. Around 150 years after Shakespeare died, New Place was acquired as a summer home by Reverend Francis Gastrell, vicar of Frodsham in Cheshire. By 1756 Stratford was becoming a popular destination for tourists. Gastrell became so fed up with strangers milling around his garden and breaking twigs off the famous mulberry, that he chopped it down, in what the eighteenth-century biographer James Boswell described as an act of 'gothick barbarity'.[57] Angered by the loss of their priceless local heritage, a crowd of locals gathered outside Gastrell's house and broke some of his windows. But the story gets worse. The Stratford authorities turned down Gastrell's application to extend his garden – and also demanded a full year's taxes, even though he protested that he only spent summers there. In 1759, in a fit of pique, the vicar demolished the house and fled the town not long after.[58]

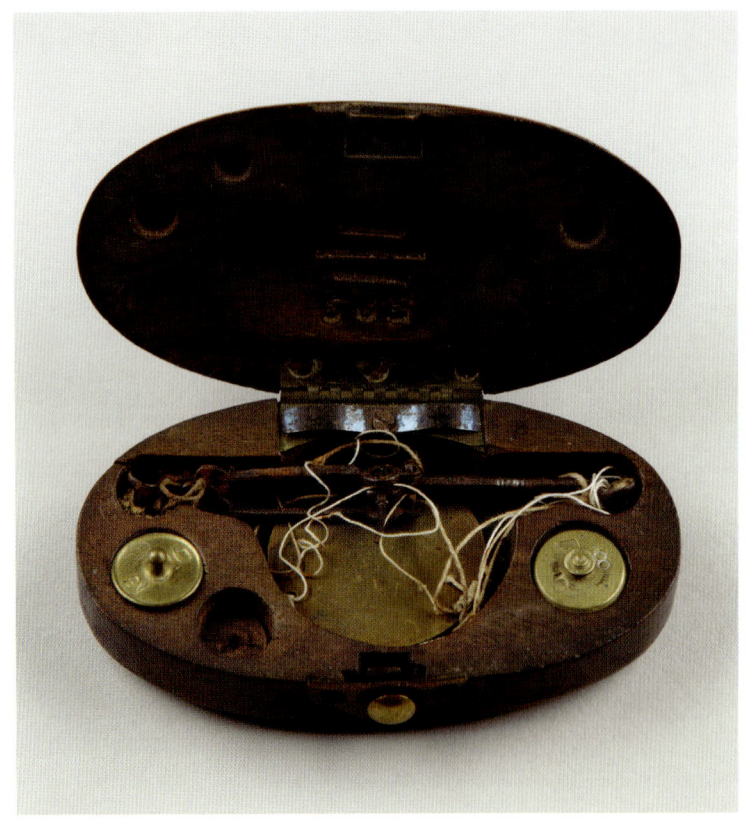

Portable scales made of wood from William Shakespeare's mulberry tree in Stratford.

Fortunately, most of the wood came into the hands of a local watchmaker and craftsman called Thomas Sharp, and other makers, George Cooper and John Marshall. Apart from Garrick's casket and goblet, the wood was used to make small memento mori, such as snuffboxes, buttons and even a small pair of scales. The wood was also incorporated into larger items, including a tabletop bearing the initials WSMT (William Shakespeare's mulberry tree) and the date 1609.

But the market for these items encouraged a lucrative counterfeit industry; some items – even those in collections today – were not even made of mulberry wood, let alone from Shakespeare's tree. As Bowe points out, 'there are far more objects claimed to be made from wood from Shakespeare's mulberry than could possibly have come from a single tree.'[59]

The Most Expensive Wood in the World

In Japan, the white mulberry is relatively common and there is a long tradition of using its timber for furniture. The most highly prized of all, though, is a unique kind of mulberry wood that is only found in the mountainous areas of a small group of volcanic islands southeast of Tokyo. Timber from these 'island mulberries' is known as *shimakuwa* (*shima* means island and *kuwa* means mulberry) and has a complex grain structure that can produce exquisite results.

Shimakuwa is especially associated with two of the beautiful Izu islands, Mikurajima and Miyakejima, which, while idyllic, can have dangerously high levels of sulphur dioxide from smoking, active volcanoes. Miyakejima had to be evacuated in 2000 because of the fumes, earning it the sobriquet 'gas mask island'.

The mulberry species used for *shimakuwa* is *Morus kagayama Koidz*, which is in fact a common species of white mulberry found throughout East Asia, where it is known as *Morus bombycis* or *M. australis* (Chinese mulberry or Korean mulberry). However, the timber from Izu island trees, which can be over 1,000 years old, has acquired characteristics found in no other wood, precisely because of the environmental stress caused by the toxic atmosphere, as Bowe explains:

> The wood often has a three-dimensional character in which the lower grain appears like water into which a stone has been dropped – with interesting patterns and convolutions. The colour has been described as a combination of silver/gold – with the wood glowing and exhibiting *chatoyance* – rather like the semi-precious gemstone Tigers Eye [Pietersite].[60]

Chatoyance, which is a corruption of the French *oeil de chat* or cat's eye, refers to a unique property whereby cavities and minerals below

Veteran *shimakuwa* mulberry tree on the volcanic island of Mikurajima (Japan) – the most expensive wood in the world?

Tree of Plenty

the surface reflect light, causing a silk-like sheen and a luminous band of highlight that moves as the object is moved.

Shimakuwa wood is particularly valued for some of the many objects associated with the tea ceremony, including tea caddies, spoons and chopsticks. It is also used to make *netsuke*, small carved toggles to fasten pouches worn over traditional clothes, instead of pockets. This unusual wood was favoured by furniture makers in the Edo period (1603–1868), particularly within the *sashimono* tradition, which uses complex joints to fix the component pieces, rather than metal screws or nails. At one time, *shimakuwa* timber was reserved to make furniture and other wooden objects for the Japanese royal family.

Specialized master makers still use Izu island *shimakuwa* mulberry wood for modern, Edo-style *sashimono* furniture, but it has become extremely difficult to source. With the population of Izu trees declining and sometimes in poor health, the species has become protected. Some of the makers still have reserve supplies but are now more likely to use it for smaller objects, further pushing up the price of larger *sashimono* furniture. Today, the craftsmen who make this furniture are

Flat chess-piece box in highly prized *shimakuwa* mulberry wood by Kyoshi Ishimushi, showing chatoyance.

Master craftsman in the Kichizo workshop, Japan.

considered national treasures in Japan, while the *shimakuwa* mulberry has become the most expensive wood in the world.[61]

Mulberry as a Landscape Tree

Apart from the multiple uses for all parts of the mulberry, the trees have long been grown simply for their unique beauty and the shade they provide. Black mulberries, in particular, look ancient even when they are just fifty years old. Their gnarled, leaning trunks, heavy drooping branches and spreading canopy give them an ornamental value that is hard to equal. As the former curator of the Royal Botanic Gardens at Kew, William Bean, put it, 'nothing gives to a garden fortunate enough to possess it a greater sense of old-world charm and dignity than a rugged old mulberry standing on a lawn.'[62]

Tree of Plenty

Black mulberries were planted at each of the four corners of the West Garden at Hatfield House, either by Robert Cecil's gardener, John Tradescant the Elder, shortly after Cecil received the house from James I in 1607, or during Elizabeth I's years there as a child, until she took up the throne in 1558. Only one of these mulberries survives, as a squat, pollarded tree with a hollow trunk – but it is in excellent health.

For Queen Victoria's Golden Jubilee, four black mulberries were planted in the secluded Fountain Court in Middle Temple, one of the Inns of Court hidden behind high walls off the Strand in the City of London. Two have survived and are now leaning towards the fountain, supported on props. West Square (named after the Temple West family who owned the land), in Southwark, south of the Thames, was laid out around 1799 and also featured four black mulberries. Three survive today, growing almost horizontally and supported on props. Several white mulberries have more recently been added to the garden.

Kichizo *sashimono* sewing box in *shimakuwa* (Izu island mulberry wood), 20th century.

Several other public parks in London include a black mulberry, planted when they were laid out in Victorian times, as part of a fashion for arboreta – including as many tree species as possible in a new park. Several royal parks have mulberry trees, too: Kensington Gardens has a double row of mulberries, those on one side being *M. nigra*, and on the other side, *M. alba*; Windsor Castle has an avenue of black mulberries, planted in the nineteenth century for Queen Victoria; and, of course, the 35 mulberry trees of the UK National Mulberry Collection growing in the gardens of Buckingham Palace also serve a decorative function as landscape trees, even though several are still saplings. The Royal Botanical Gardens at Kew, Chelsea Physic Garden, the Oxford Botanical Garden and Edinburgh Botanical Garden all contain fine examples of mulberries.

New York's Central Park is home to several mulberry trees, both white and black, which are the focus for foraging in summer. A row of white mulberry trees has been planted in the Tuileries gardens in Paris, inside the railings by the rue de Rivoli, roughly where Henri IV had planted a double row four hundred years ago. There were once hundreds, if not thousands, of mulberries in the parks of the Swabian and Norman rulers of Sicily in the Middle Ages.

When James I tried to get earls and lords to plant mulberries for silk in the grounds of their houses up and down the country, some took up the offer. We have little idea on what scale they were planted but, when the project failed, not all of the trees were grubbed out. The result is a legacy of dozens of old black mulberry trees around Britain. As Scottish botanist and garden designer John Claudius Loudon wrote: 'there is scarcely an old garden or gentleman's seat, throughout the country, which can be traced back to the seventeenth century, in which a mulberry tree is not to be found.'[63]

Archaeological Markers

Several of these old trees still survive, mostly because their owners appreciate their unique ornamental value. Stephen Bowe made a painstaking effort to trace survivors of James I's sericultural project in a postal survey for his *Mulberry* book, published in 2015. On the basis of the responses he received, he was able to compile an inventory of over a hundred veteran mulberries. In some cases, such as Christ's College, Cambridge, there are records of mulberry trees being purchased in 1609 – along with material to build a silkworm house – expressly to support the king's sericulture project.

The black mulberry offers generous shade and an abundance of fruit. Engraving by the British satirical artist George Cruikshank, 1808.

Black mulberry at Christ's College, Cambridge, planted in 1609. The poet Milton would have known the young tree when he was a student there from 1624.

In 2016–17 the UK's *Morus Londinium* project, initiated by the author, complemented this work with an online survey of mulberry trees of all ages in Greater London (and, in fact, beyond) and brought to light over 350 old trees, many hidden from view in private gardens. In several cases these trees were preserved when mansion houses were sold off and developed in the great Victorian urban expansion of the latter part of the nineteenth century. It is a tribute to the affection that people have for old mulberries – as well as the foresight of municipal councils – that these trees have been protected.

These surviving trees now serve a new purpose – as archaeological markers for research into the lost heritage of urban areas that have seen massive development. Starting with an old mulberry in an unlikely place, such as a street corner or back garden, archival research often reveals a hidden past, when the tree was growing in the grounds of a mansion, school, monastery or even as part of an orchard or mulberry plantation. Interest in these old trees is such that most are now protected from destruction. When one is threatened, it can mobilize local residents to stop a planned development. These mulberries have acquired the status of local landmarks.

This veneration for old (mulberry) trees is by no means only a British trait. From India and Japan to the Middle East, Italy, Spain, France and the U.S., veteran mulberries are treasured for their inherent beauty, as well as their landmark value as monuments to a distant past. Not only have they already outlived generations of rulers (totalitarian or otherwise) and ordinary people, but many of the buildings that they were planted next to as well. We often think of the oak or the yew as ancient landmark trees, but perhaps the time has come for the humble mulberry, unshackled from its 5,000 years of bondage to the silkworm, to take its place alongside them.

Timeline

63.5 million years ago (MYA)	*Morus* genus first appears
2.6 MYA	Pleistocene period begins: Ice Ages reduce forest cover
11,700 years ago	End of Ice Ages: temperate forests appear
4000 BCE	Ivory cup with silkworm design made in Zhejiang province (China)
2700 BCE	Origin of Chinese sericulture in Shangdong. Silk ribbons, threads and woven fragments found at Qianshanyang in Huzhou, Zhejiang province
2640 BCE	Legend of first sericulturalist discovering silk
2600–2300 BCE	Silkworm cocoon cut in half at Yangshao culture site on the Yellow River in Shanxi province
2450 BCE	Evidence of 'tussah' silk made in Indus Valley using wild *Antheraea* moths feeding on native forest trees
1600–1046 BCE	Shang dynasty. Chinese already cultivating the native *M. alba*
First millennium BCE	Chinese peoples move southwards from Yellow River
1046–256 BCE	Zhou period: folk songs refer to silk weaving

Timeline

800 BCE	Seedling of *Morus boninensis* mulberry tree found on Ogasawara Islands (Japan) starts to grow
594 BCE	Lu state of Zhou dynasty (China) levies tax on inherited mulberry fields
476–225 BCE	Warring States period: women use mulberry hooks in sericulture
6th–5th centuries BCE	Ancient Greeks aware of silk and sericulture. Ezekiel mentions *amorgis* in Babylon
384–322 BCE	Aristotle writes of silkworm in *History of Animals*
371–287 BCE	Greek philosopher Theophrastus distinguishes mulberry (*sykaminos*) from sycamore (*sykaminos Aegyptia*)
350 BCE	New Comedy poets write on black mulberry juice to paint cheeks
206 BCE–220 CE	Han dynasty in China
206 BCE–9 CE	*Fan Shengzhi shu* details mulberry cultivation techniques
138 BCE	Han dynasty seizes potential for trade between China and Central Asia
2nd century BCE	Chinese migrants introduce sericulture to Korean peninsula
70–19 BCE	Roman poet Virgil writes about sericulture
65–8 BCE	Roman poet Horace writes about black mulberry fruit
58 BCE	Julius Caesar invades Gaul (now southern France)
1st century BCE	Romans introduce *Morus nigra* to France
43 BCE–17 CE	Roman poet Ovid writes *Pyramus and Thisbe*
25 BCE–220 CE	Eastern Han dynasty: sericulture shifts to Yangtze River basin
14–37 CE	Roman emperor Tiberius passes sumptuary laws on wearing silk

23–79 CE	Pliny the Elder writes on mulberries and silk production
43–84 CE	Roman invasion of England
1st–2nd century CE	Romans introduce *Morus nigra* to England
105 CE	Cai Lun makes mulberry bark paper in Han dynasty China
110–80 CE	Pausanias writes on 'people of Seres', silk and silkworms
150–350 CE	Sericulture in Khotan (Tarim basin) using *M. alba*
224–641 CE	Sassanid Persian Empire
260 CE	City state of Samarkand (now in Uzbekistan) becomes major hub for trade – and possibly sericulture
330 CE	Constantine I moves Roman capital to Byzantium, renames it Constantinople
386–534 CE	Northern Wei dynasty: farmers must plant fifty mulberry trees for every 5 acres (2 ha) of farmland provided by the government
410 CE	Romans leave England
486 CE	Romans leave Gaul
500–640 CE	*Bombyx* sericulture introduced to Sassanid Persia using *M. nigra*
527 CE	Justinian I becomes ruler of Byzantine Empire
533–44 CE	Chapter on mulberry cultivation in Chinese text, *Qimin Yaoshu*
550 CE	Turkish Bulgar peoples take control of the area from Black Sea to Chinese frontier
552 CE	*M. Bombyx* sericulture introduced to Byzantium using *nigra*

Timeline

7th century CE	Afghan *rubab* lute made from mulberry wood
7th–8th centuries CE	Islamic conquests of Central Asia. Votive panel shows princess in her headdress introducing sericulture to Khotan
618–907 CE	Tang dynasty: earliest paper money
622–32 CE	Islamic rule expands throughout Arabian peninsula
706 CE	Oldest known woodblock print of Great Dharani Sutra of Undefiled Pure Radiance made on mulberry paper
711–88 CE	Umayyad caliphate introduces *M. nigra* and sericulture to Iberian peninsula
751 CE	Islamic army defeats Chinese Tang army in the Talas Valley
802 CE	Charlemagne includes black mulberries in his Capitulary
868 CE	Diamond Sutra produced on mulberry paper, discovered by Wang Yuanlu in cave library in Dunhuang (China) in 1900
918–1392 CE	Goryeo kingdom in Korean peninsula – *hanji* mulberry paper reaches a peak of renown.
960–1127 CE	Sung dynasty China: planting mulberries is a criterion for civil service promotion
10th century CE	Text by Su Yijian confirms that mulberry bark (*sang-phi*) used in north of China for paper-making. Constantinople is now a major silk-manufacturing centre
12th century CE	Roger II's Kingdom of Sicily includes most of Italy south of Rome. Rise of sericulture in southern Italy
1147 CE	General George Maniakes of Sicily launches attacks on Peloponnese peninsula and city of Thebes, captures skilled silk workers

1170 CE	Murder of Thomas Becket in Canterbury cathedral: mulberry tree mentioned by Gervase, who was a witness
1204 CE	Sack of Constantinople in Fourth Crusade
1219–25 CE	Mongol conquests destroy sericulture irrigation in Central Asia
1271–95 CE	Marco Polo travels to Khanbaliq (Beijing) and stays with Kublai Khan
13th century CE	*M. nigra* planted for sericulture in Comtat Venaissin (France)
1368–1644 CE	Ming dynasty (China) farmers required to plant six hundred trees in three years
1434 CE	Francesco Buonvicino introduces *M. alba* to Pescia (northern Italy)
1441 CE	Florentine authorities require peasant farmers to plant 3–50 mulberries per year
1453 CE	Fall of Constantinople to Ottoman Empire
1466 CE	Louis XI (1423–1483) seeks to encourage silk industry in Lyons
1481 CE	Nello di Francesco plants 10,000 mulberries in Siena.
1483–98 CE	Charles VIII encourages sericulture in France
1492 CE	Alhambra decree forces Jews to convert to Catholicism or leave Spain
1494 CE	Guy-Pape de Saint-Auban plants first *M. alba* in France
1531	Spanish colonizers find *Morus rubra* in Oaxaca (Mexico) and introduce *Bombyx mori* for sericulture
1536–41	Henry VIII and his first minister, Thomas Cromwell, dissolve Catholic monasteries in England

1540	François I grants Lyons a monopoly on imports of raw silk
1548	William Turner records seeing M. *nigra* at Syon House near London
1550	Italian silk makes up 30 per cent of French imports and 20 per cent of imports to the Low Countries
1554	Henri II promulgates first statutes governing manufacture of silk in France
1561	Joseph Nasi starts sericulture on the shores of the Sea of Galilee
1572	St Bartholomew's Day massacre in France of 10,000 Huguenots, including silk weavers
1589–1610	Henri IV of Navarre (1589–1610) supports French sericulture
1594–5	Shakespeare writes of mulberry in *A Midsummer Night's Dream*
1596	François Traucat starts nursery for M. *alba* trees in Nîmes
1597	Shakespeare purchases New Place in Stratford-upon-Avon, which has a black mulberry tree. John Gerard's *Herbal* mentions mulberries
1599	Henri IV asks landowners to plant white mulberries around their houses
1598	Louis XIV revokes Edict of Nantes. Huguenot weavers flee, notably to England and Netherlands
1601	Olivier de Serres plants 15–20,000 M. *alba* trees in the Jardin des Tuileries, next to Henri IV's Louvre Palace in Paris
1602	Jean-Baptiste Letellier publishes manual on sericulture in French

1603–1868	Edo period in Japan: *Sashimono* tradition uses mulberry wood for Imperial tea ceremony objects and furniture
1604	Vicenza produces 120,000 light pounds (about 72,600 kg, or 160,000 lb) of silk
1605–9	William Shakespeare writes of the fragility of the ripe mulberry in *Coriolanus*
1607	James I writes to lord lieutenants asking them to plant 10,000 mulberries to start a silk industry in England. Imports 100,000 *M. nigra* saplings. James plants 10,000 trees in grounds of St James's Palace, Greenwich, Theobalds and Oatlands. Nicholas Geffe translates into English a French manual by Olivier de Serres on sericulture. It is published by William Stallenge
1607–9	First attempts at sericulture in Virginia using native *M. rubra*
1608	River Thames freezes over. Several frost fairs on Thames during seventeenth century. Britain is passing through Little Ice Age
1609	Four Cambridge colleges (Christ's, Corpus Christi, Emmanuel and Jesus) plant *M. nigra* for sericulture
1610	Henri IV assassinated by a Catholic fanatic
1611	Charlton House near Greenwich completed as residence for the tutor to James I's son Henry. Mulberries planted for sericulture
1623	A Virginia farmer could be fined 10 livres if he did not plant at least ten (red) mulberry trees
1629	First *M. rubra* (red mulberry) planted in England
1630	Charles I appoints John Tradescant the Elder as keeper of king's silkworms and mulberries
1639	Sir Francis Wyatt recommends planting *M. alba* for sericulture in Virginia rather than native *M. rubra*

Timeline

1644–1911	Qing dynasty: extensive mulberry cultivation for Chinese sericulture
1652	Louis XIV abolishes taxes on silk made in Lyons
1654	Louis XIV builds Palace of Versailles
1656	Louis XIV grants letters patent to Jean Hindret to use the Madrid palace (west of Paris) for sericulture and a silk stocking factory
1660	Restoration of Charles II, who promotes sericulture in England
1664	John Evelyn publishes *Sylva, or a Discourse of Forest-trees and the Propagation of Timber*
1668	Samuel Pepys writes of Mulberry Garden in London
1682	The explorers Henri de Tonti and Sieur de la Salle find old men in a Natchez village dressed in cloaks made from the inner bark of the red mulberry
1685	Louis XIV promulgates Edict of Fontainebleau, revoking Edict of Nantes and precipitating exodus of Huguenot weavers, notably to England and Netherlands
1720–23	Raw Silk Company mulberry plantation in Chelsea (London)
1722–3	Plague decimates Avignon's silk workers
1725	Sericulture starts in Pennsylvania
1732	Sericulture starts in Georgia
1740s	Frederick II of Prussia encourages planting of mulberry trees.
1752	Silk weavers of Lyons complain of shortage of mulberry trees for local sericulture
1755	South Carolina plantation-owner, Eliza Lucas Pinckney, takes enough of her own silk to England to make three dresses

1756	Prussian decree forbids import of foreign silk. Reverend Gastrell fells Shakespeare's mulberry tree in Stratford-upon-Avon
1759	Savannah (Georgia) silk-reeling mill receives 4,535 kg (10,000 lb) of home-grown raw silk cocoons
1763	Matthieu Thomé of the Royal Agricultural Society of Lyons vows to rescue French sericulture from 'degradation'
1769	Casket presented to actor David Garrick, made of wood from Shakespeare's black mulberry tree
1776	War of Independence deals a blow to American sericulture
1821	French botanist Georges Guerrard-Samuel Perrottet finds a new variety of white mulberry, *Morus alba multicaulis*, in the Philippines
1823	Samuel Whitmarsh causes rush in demand for *M. multicaulis* slips in America
1824	Silk looms of Lyons working day and night again
1829	A Monsieur Combet records having 40,000 mulberries on land near Vincennes (Paris)
1836	10,000 *M. alba* trees recorded growing in Neuilly (Paris)
1840	France produces 26,000 tonnes of silk
1845	*Pébrine* (silkworm disease) first recorded in France and spreads throughout Europe
1850	Savannah becomes a leading centre for silk production
1853	Capt. Perry visits Bonin (Ogasawara) Islands and discovers 2,800-year-old white mulberries (*M. boninensis*)
1865	Production of silk in France plummets to 4,000 tonnes

Timeline

1872	Suez Canal opens, giving boost to Japanese silk exports
1889	Vincent van Gogh paints mulberry tree at Saint-Rémy (France), a year before his suicide
1900–1917	Sir Aurel Stein excavates ancient sites in Central Asia and finds fossilized mulberry trees in Taklamakan Desert
1929	Wall Street stock market crash
1930s	Over 40 per cent of Japanese farmers employed in sericulture
1932	Zoe Lady Hart Dyke starts what becomes Lullingstone Silk Farm in England
1958	Crayola crayon company adds 'mulberry' to its colour range
1986	Chinese artist Liang Shaoji uses life-cycle of the silkworm in his art
2012	'Craftsmanship and Performance Art of the Azerbaijani Tar' (using mulberry wood) inscribed on the UNESCO List of Intangible Cultural Heritage
2014	Gunma silk factory site (Japan) inscribed on the UNESCO World Heritage List
2017	Japan's Kumamoto Prefecture opens a U.S.$21 million 'bioclean' silkworm factory in what it calls 'Silk on Valley'

References

Introduction

1 Figures for 2013: UN Food and Agriculture Organization, 'FAO Value of Agricultural Production', http://knoema.com/FAOVAP2015Feb/fao-value-of-agricultural-production-february-2015, accessed 25 November 2015.
2 As James A. Millward, author of *The Silk Road: A Very Short Introduction* (Oxford and New York, 2013), has put it: 'Neither silk, nor a road.'
3 Susan Whitfield, *Silk, Slaves, and Stupas* (Oakland, CA, 2018).
4 As distinct from weaving silk fabric, which is a much older practice.
5 'Adi Shankar's Ancient Mulberry', *Landmark Trees of India*, https://outreachecology.com/landmark (November 2012). Peter Smetacek, 'A Tree Created in India', *Times of India* 20 May 2007.
6 Stephen J. Bowe, *Mulberry: The Material Culture of Mulberry Trees* (Liverpool, 2015).
7 Alan Mitchell, 'Facts about Mulberries', *The Garden*, CIV (December 1984), pp. 514–15.
8 Caroline R. Cartwright, Christina M. Duffy and Helen Wang, 'Microscopical Examination of Fibres used in Ming Dynasty Paper Money', *Technical Research Bulletin*, VIII (2014), pp. 105–16.

1 Black, White and Red

1 A database of plant names maintained by the Royal Botanic Gardens at Kew (UK) and the Missouri Botanical Garden (U.S.), www.theplantlist.org.
2 Qiwei Zeg et al., 'Definition of Eight Mulberry Species in the Genus *Morus* by Internal Transcribed Spacer-based Phylogeny', *PLoS ONE* (12 August 2015), https://doi.org/10.1371/journal.pone.0135411.
3 Olivier de Serres, *La cueillete de la soye par la nourriture des Vers qui la font. Echantillon du Théâtre d'Agriculture d'Olivier de Serres Seigneur du Pradel* [1599] (Paris, 1843).

4 Geffe borrowed heavily from another text in French by Jean-Baptiste Letellier, entitled *Memoires et instructions pour l'establissement des meuriers, et art de faire la soye en France* (Paris, 1603).
5 Olivier de Serres, *The Perfect Use of Silk-wormes, and their Benefit*, trans. Nicholas Geffe (London, 1607), pp. 20–21.
6 William Jackson Bean, *Trees and Shrubs, Hardy in the British Isles* [1914] (London, 1936), vol. II, p. 85.
7 Pliny (the Elder), *Natural History*, trans. H. Rackham (London, 1945), vol. IV, book XVI, p. 455.
8 Edward Augustus 'Gussie' Bowles, *My Garden in Spring* (London, 1914).
9 Jon Dean, personal communication, March 2018.
10 Victor Hehn, *Cultivated Plants and Domesticated Animals in their Migration from Asia to Europe* (London, 1885), p. 293.
11 John Gerard, *The Herball; or, Generall Historie of Plantes* (London, 1597), book III, p. 1324.
12 William Turner, *A New Herball Parts II and III* [1568], ed. George T. L. Chapman et al. (Cambridge, 1995), p. 139.
13 Miles Hadfield, 'Growing Mulberries in Britain', *Country Life* (13 September 1962), p. 578.
14 Hehn, *Cultivated Plants*, p. 293.
15 Horace, *Satire IV: The Works of Horace in Latin and English* (London, 1718), book II, p. 465.
16 Peter Thomas, personal communication, January 2013.
17 Barrie Juniper, 'The Mysterious Origin of the Sweet Apple', *American Scientist*, XCV (2007), pp. 44–51.
18 M. Modzelevich, *Flowers in Israel*, www.flowersinisrael.com, accessed 11 August 2018.
19 Wilhelmina F. Jashemski and Frederick G. Meyer, *The Natural History of Pompeii* (Cambridge, 2002), pp. 126–7.
20 Erica Rowan, 'Bioarchaeological Preservation and Non-elite Diet in the Bay of Naples: An Analysis of the Food Remains from the Cardo V Sewer at the Roman Site of Herculaneum', *Environmental Archaeology*, XX (2017), pp. 318–36.
21 Gaius Plinius Caecilius Secundus, *Letters of Pliny*, trans. William Melmoth, Project Gutenberg (2001), www.gutenberg.org, accessed 22 March 2019.
22 Mark Travis, 'Why Grow Mulberries?', www.growingmulberry.org, accessed 8 July 2017.
23 Pliny the Elder, *Natural History* (London, 1945), vol. IV, book XV, p. 355.
24 Bean, *Trees and Shrubs*, vol. II, p. 86.
25 Hadfield, 'Growing Mulberries in Britain', p. 293.
26 Karen Liljenberg, *London's Lost Garden*, https://londonslostgarden.wordpress.com, accessed 14 August 2014.
27 Gerard, *The Herball*, p. 1324.
28 Scott Leathart, *Whence Our Trees* (London, 1991), pp. 184–6.

29 Matthew C. Perry, *Narrative of an expedition of an American squadron to the China seas and Japan under the command of Commodore M. C. Perry, United States Navy* (Washington, DC, 1856), p. 210.
30 *M. boninensis* is tetraploid – it has four sets of chromosomes – while *M. alba* typically has just two, that is, it is diploid.
31 Naoki Tani et al., 'Determination of the Genetic Structure of Remnant *Morus boninensis Koidz* Trees to Establish a Conservation Program on the Bonin Islands, Japan', *BMC Ecology*, VI (2006), https://doi.org, accessed 18 February 2019.
32 Hehn, *Cultivated Plants*, p. 487, n. 73.
33 Dieter Kuhn, 'Textile Technology: Spinning and Reeling', in *Science and Civilization in China*, vol. V: *Chemistry and Chemical Technology; Part IX*, ed. Joseph Needham (Cambridge, 1988), p. 289.
34 J. Swearingen and C. Bargeron, *Invasive Plant Atlas of the United States*, www.invasiveplantatlas.com, accessed 13 August 2018.
35 Serres, *The Perfect Use of Silk-wormes*, p. 20.
36 Paul Peacock, 'Going Round the Mulberry Bush', *Grow It!* (July 2007), pp. 36–7.
37 With mirror collections at Windsor Palace and Kensington Palace gardens.
38 Susyn Andrews, John Feltwell, Mark Lane and Alysia Hunt, *The Queen's Mulberries* (London, 2012).
39 Philip E. Taylor et al., 'High-speed pollen release in the white mulberry tree, *Morus alba* L.', *Sexual Plant Reproduction*, XIX (March 2006), pp. 19–24.
40 This startling phenomenon can be seen in many amateur videos published on YouTube, for example: Philip Taylor, 'Fast Plants: Morus alba', accessed 18 February 2019.
41 William Bartram, *Travels of William Bartram* [1791] (Philadelphia, PA, 1928), pp. 57, 25.
42 COSEWIC, 'Assessment and Status Report on the Red Mulberry *Morus rubra* in Canada', Species at Risk Public Registry, http://sararegistry.gc.ca (11 December 2015).
43 Katherine Gould, Angela Steward and Steven D. Glenn, 'Morus', *New York Metropolitan Flora Project*, www.bbg.org/collections/nymf, accessed 1 October 2018.
44 John Claudius Loudon, *Arboretum et Fruticetum Britannicum; or, The Trees and Shrubs of Britain* (London, 1844), vol. III, p. 1360.
45 Bean, *Trees and Shrubs*, vol. II, p. 86.
46 Loudon, *Arboretum et Fruticetum*, vol. III, p. 1361.
47 William Jackson Bean, *Trees and Shrubs, Hardy in the British Isles* (London, 1914), vol. I, p. 267.
48 Loudon, *Arboretum et Fruticetum*, vol. III, p. 1361.
49 Bean, *Trees and Shrubs*, vol. I, p. 268.
50 Robert Birsel, 'Mulberry trees bring misery to Pakistani city', *Health News*, www.reuters.com (5 March 2007).

2 Mulberries and Silk

1 Dieter Kuhn, 'Textile Technology: Spinning and Reeling', in *Science and Civilisation in China*, vol. V: *Chemistry and Chemical Technology*, ed. Joseph Needham (Cambridge, 1988), part IX, p. 248.
2 William F. Leggett, *The Story of Silk* (New York, 1949).
3 Kuhn, 'Textile Technology', p. 248.
4 Yongkang Huo, 'Mulberry Cultivation and Utilization in China' (FAO Electronic Conference on Mulberry for Animal Production (Morus-L), Rome, 2002), www.fao.org, accessed 19 February 2019.
5 Figures for 2013: UN Food and Agriculture Organization, see http://knoema.com/FAOVAP2015Feb/fao-value-of-agricultural-production-february-2015, accessed 25 November 2015. Other sources put the figure much higher – see www.tradeforum.org/Silk-in-World-Markets, accessed 9 May 2017.
6 Irene Good, 'The Archaeology of Early Silk', *Textile Society of America Symposium Proceedings* (2002), pp. 7–15.
7 Frances Carey, *The Tree: Meaning and Myth* (London, 2012), p. 124.
8 Kuhn, 'Textile Technology', p. 286.
9 Liu Zhijuan, *The Story of Silk* (Beijing, 2006).
10 Good, 'The Archaeology of Early Silk', pp. 7–15.
11 David L. Wood, Robert M. Silverstein and Minoru Nakajima, eds, *Control of Insect Behavior by Natural Products* (New York, San Francisco, CA, and London, 1970).
12 K. Konno et al., 'Mulberry Latex Rich in Antidiabetic Sugar-mimic Alkaloids Forces Dieting on Caterpillars', *Proceedings of the National Academy of Sceinces*, CIII (31 January 2006), pp. 1337–41.
13 Kuhn, 'Textile Technology', p. 274.
14 Claudio Zanier, *Where the Roads Meet* (Kyoto, 1994).
15 Charles Stevens and Jean Liebault, *The Third Booke of the Countrey Farme*, trans. Richard Surflet and updated by Gervase Markham (London, 1616), p. 488.
16 Ibid.
17 Jean-Baptiste Letellier, *Instructions for the increasing of mulberie trees, and the breeding of silke-wormes, for the making of silke in this kingdome*, trans. William Stallenge (London, 1609).
18 Stevens and Liebault, *Countrey Farme*, p. 489.
19 K. P. Arunkumar, Muralidhar Metta and J. Nagaraju, 'Molecular Phylogeny of Silkmoths Reveals the Origin of Domesticated Silkmoth, *Bombyx mori* from Chinese *Bombyx mandarina* and Paternal Inheritance of Mitochondrial DNA', *Molecular Phylogenetics and Evolution*, XL (August 2006), pp. 419–27.
20 'Captive Breeding for Thousands of Years has Impaired Olfactory Functions in Silkmoths', *Max Planck Society*, www.mpg.de (21 November 2013).
21 Dietrich Schneider, 'Pheromone Communication in Moths and Butterflies', in *Sensory Physiology and Behavior, Advances in Behavioral Biology*,

ed. R. Galun, P. Hillam, L. Parnas and R. Werman (Boston, MA, 1975), vol. XV, pp. 173–93.
22 Ningjia He et al., 'Draft Genome Sequence of the Mulberry Tree *Morus notabilis*', *Nature Communications* (19 September 2013).
23 MiRNAs play a key role in determining whether or not given genes are expressed.
24 Krishna Riboud, 'A Closer View of Early Chinese Silks', in *Studies in Textile History*, ed. Veronika Gervers (Ontario, 1977), pp. 252–80.
25 Kuhn, 'Textile Technology', p. 279.
26 Ibid., p. 200.
27 Irene Good, Jonathan M. Kenoyer and Richard Meadow, 'New Evidence for Early Silk in the Indus Civilization', *Archaeometry*, L (2009), pp. 457–66.
28 Irene Good, 'On the Question of Silk in Pre-Han Eurasia', *Antiquity*, LXIX (1995), pp. 959–68.
29 Ibid.
30 Xinru Liu, *The Silk Road in World History* (Oxford, 2010).
31 Kuhn, 'Textile Technology', p. 285.
32 Ibid., p. 294.
33 Leggett, *The Story of Silk*, pp. 74–5.
34 Susan Whitfield, *Silk, Slaves, and Stupas* (Oakland, CA, 2018), p. 194.
35 Leggett, *The Story of Silk*.
36 Manfred G. Raschke, 'New Studies in Roman Commerce with the East', in *Aufstieg und Niedergang der Römischen Welt, Geschichte und Kultur Roms in der neueren Forschung*, ed. Hildegard Temporini (Berlin, 1978), vol. IX, pp. 604–1361.
37 Good, 'On the Question of Silk', p. 963.
38 Raschke, 'New Studies in Roman Commerce', pp. 604ff.
39 Susan Whitfield, *Life Along the Silk Road* (London, 1999), p. 9.
40 Aurel Stein, *Ancient Khotan* (Oxford, 1907), vol. I, p. 229.
41 Ibid.
42 Peter Hopkirk, *Foreign Devils on the Silk Road: The Search for the Lost Treasures of Central Asia* (Oxford, 2001), p. 12.
43 Liu, *Silk Road in World History*, p. 12.
44 Pliny the Elder, *Natural History*, trans. John Bostock and H. T. Riley (London, 1855), vol. III, book XI, pp. 26–7, n. 86.
45 Gisela M. A. Richter, 'Silk in Greece', *American Journal of Archaeology*, XXXIII (1929), pp. 27–33.
46 A 'hackle' is a comb, used for flax. It is also a coxcomb and the hairs that rise on an animal's back when it is frightened.
47 See Richter, 'Silk in Greece'.
48 William T. M. Forbes, 'The Silkworm of Aristotle', *Classical Philology*, XXV (January 1930), pp. 22–6. See also http://penelope.uchicago.edu/aristotle/histanimals5.htm, accessed 17 January 2018.
49 Pliny, *Natural History*, vol. III, p. 26.
50 Cited in Liu, *Silk Road in World History*, p. 20.

51 Cited in *Archives Historiques et Statistiques du Département du Rhône* (Lyons, 1825), vol. II, p. 298. Translation author's own.
52 Cited in Olivier de Serres, *The Perfect Use of Silk-wormes, and their Benefit*, trans. Nicholas Geffe (London, 1607), p. 2.
53 Cited in *Archives Historiques*, vol. II, p. 297.
54 Liu, *Silk Road in World History*, p. 74.
55 Cited in *Procopius: The Roman Silk Industry c. 550*, https://sourcebooks.fordham.edu, accessed 6 February 2018.
56 Susan Whitfield, personal communication, August 2018.
57 Zoe Lady Hart Dyke, *So Spins the Silkworm* (London, 1949).
58 See Liu, *The Silk Road in World History*.
59 UNESCO has a superb online resource for further reading on the Silk Roads: https://en.unesco.org/silkroad, accessed March 2019.

3 Lost Angels

1 Edward Thomas, *In Pursuit of Spring* (London, 1914), p. 36.
2 Victor Hehn, *Cultivated Plants and Domestic Animals in their Migration from Asia to Europe* (London, 1885), p. 292.
3 Ibid.
4 Henry N. Ellacombe, *The Plant Lore and Garden Craft of Shakespeare* (London, 1896), p. 176.
5 Horace, *Satire IV: The Odes, Satyrs and Epistles of Horace*, trans. T. Creech (London, 1720), p. 249.
6 Wilhelmina Feemster Jashemski and Frederick G. Meyer, eds, *The Natural History of Pompeii* (Cambridge, 2002), p. 127.
7 Maud Grieve, *A Modern Herbal* [1931] (New York, 1971), vol. II, p. 559.
8 Joakim F. Schouw, *Die Erde, die Pflanzen und der Mensch* (Leipzig, 1854), p. 37.
9 Alexandra Livarda, 'New Temptations? Olive, Cherry and Mulberry in Roman and Medieval Europe', in *Food and Drink in Archaeology*, ed. S. Baker, M. Allen, S. Middle and K. Poole (Totnes, 2008), pp. 73–83.
10 John J. Butt, *Daily Life in the Age of Charlemagne* (London, 2002), p. 69.
11 George H. Wilcox, 'Exotic Plants from Roman Waterlogged Sites in London', *Journal of Archaeological Science*, IV/3 (1977), pp. 269–82.
12 Lisa A. Lodwick, 'The Debatable Territory where Geology and Archaeology Meet: Reassessing the Early Archaeobotanical Work of Clement Reid and Arthur Lyell at Roman Silchester', *Environmental Archaeology*, XXII (2016), pp. 56–78.
13 Marijke van der Veen, Alexandra Livarda and Alistair Hill, 'New Plant Foods in Roman Britain – Dispersal and Social Access', *Environmental Archaeology*, XII (2008), pp. 11–36.
14 Xinru Liu, *The Silk Road in World History* (Oxford, 2010), p. 101.
15 Susan Whitfield, *Silk, Slaves, and Stupas* (Oakland, CA, 2018).
16 John Claudius Loudon, *Arboretum et Frutecetum Britannicum* (London, 1844), vol. III, pp. 1342–62.

17 Alfred T. Grove and Oliver Rackham, *The Nature of Mediterranean Europe: An Ecological History* (New Haven, CT, and London, 2003), p. 316.
18 'Spanish Silk – Alpajura Secrets in Granada Province', www.piccavey.com (10 November 2015).
19 Grove and Rackham, *Nature of Mediterranean Europe*, p. 107.
20 Ibid., p. 113.
21 Leslie Grace, '460 Years of Silk in Oaxaca, Mexico', *Textile Society of America 9th Biennial Symposium* (Oakland, CA, 7–9 October 2004).
22 Arnold Krochmal, 'The Vanishing White Mulberry of Northern Greece', *Economic Botany*, VIII/2 (1954), pp. 145–51.
23 Frances Carey, *The Tree: Meaning and Myth* (London, 2012), pp. 124–9.
24 Roland de la Platrière, *Enclopédie méthodique: manufactures et arts* (Paris, 1784), vol. II, p. 47. Translation author's own.
25 Françoise Clavairolle, *Le magnan et l'arbre d'or: Regards anthropologiques* (Paris, 2003), p. 28.
26 Platrière, *Enclopédie méthodique*, p. 47.
27 Julian Forbes Laird, 'How Old is the Bethnal Green Mulberry?', www.spitalfieldslife.com (17 September 2018).
28 Olivier de Serres, *The Perfect Use of Silk-wormes, and their Benefit*, trans. Nicholas Geffe (London, 1607), appendix 3, n.p.
29 Linda Levy Peck, *Consuming Splendor: Society and Culture in Seventeenth-century England* (Cambridge, 2005), p. 1.
30 William Stallenge, *Instructions for the Increasing of Mulberrie Trees and the Breeding of Silke-worms* (London, 1609).
31 Jean-Baptiste Letellier, *Memoires et instructions pour l'establissement des meuriers, et art de faire la soye en France* (Paris, 1603).
32 Grieve, *A Modern Herbal*, p. 559.
33 Peck, *Consuming Splendor*.
34 Joan Thirsk, *Alternative Agriculture* (Oxford, 1997).
35 Nicholas Chrimes, *Cambridge: Treasure Island in the Fens* (Beijing, 2009).
36 Peck, *Consuming Splendor*.
37 Sarah Whale, personal communication with author, 17 October 2016.
38 Prudence Leith-Ross, *The John Tradescants* (London, 1984).
39 Jennifer Potter, *Strange Blooms: The Curious Lives and Adventures of the John Tradescants* (London, 2006).
40 Serres, *The Perfect Use of Silk-wormes*, p. 23.
41 Loudon, *Arboretum et Frutecetum*, p. 1343.
42 Serres, *The Perfect Use of Silk-wormes*, p. 31.
43 Helen Humphreys, *The Frozen Thames* (New York, 2007).
44 John Evelyn, *The Diary of John Evelyn*, ed. William Bray (London, 1901), vol. II, p. 285.
45 Samuel Pepys, *The Diary of Samuel Pepys*, ed. H. B. Wheatley (London, 1924), vol. VIII, p. 22.
46 Clement Walker, *Relations and Observations, Historical and Politick, Upon the Parliament begun Anno Dom. 1640, part II: Anarchia Anglicana; or, The History of Independency* (London, 1648), p. 257.

47 John Evelyn, *The Diary of John Evelyn*, ed. William Bray (London, 1907), vol. II, p. 41.
48 Thirsk, *Alternative Agriculture*.
49 Hehn, *Cultivated Plants*, p. 293.

4 Mulberry Mania

1 Wenhua Li, *Agro-ecological Farming Systems in China* (New York, 2001).
2 Cited by Li, ibid.
3 Ibid., p. 28.
4 Yongkang Huo, *Mulberry Cultivation and Utilization in China* (Rome, 2002).
5 Yingjie Wang and Y. Su, 'The Geo-pattern of Course Shifts of the Lower Yellow River', *Journal of Geographical Sciences*, XXI/6 (2011), pp. 1019–36.
6 Yingnan Xu, 'Industrialization and the Chinese Hand-reeled Silk Industry (1880–1930)', *Penn History Review*, XIX/1 (Autumn 2011).
7 Robert Fortune, *A Residence Among the Chinese* [1867] (London, 2006).
8 Marco Polo, *The Travels* [*c.* 1300], trans. Nigel Cliff (London, 2015), p. 143.
9 Ibid., p. 146.
10 H. Khomidy, 'Uzbekistan National Sericulture Development Plan', www.bacsa-silk.org, accessed 29 September 2018.
11 Luciano Cappellozza, 'Mulberry Germplasm Resources in Italy', www.fao.org, accessed 27 February 2018.
12 Rebecca Woodward Wendelken, 'Wefts and Worms: The Spread of Sericulture and Silk Weaving in the West before 1300', in *Medieval Clothing and Textiles*, ed. R. Netherton and G. Owen-Crocker (Woodbridge, 2014), vol. X, p. 74.
13 Olivier de Serres, *Le théâtre de l'agriculture et mésnage des champs* (Paris, 1605), p. 466. Translation author's own.
14 William Baker and William Clarke, *The Letters of Wilkie Collins*, vol. I: *1838–1865* (London, 1999), p. 104.
15 Luca Mola, *The Silk Industry of Renaissance Venice* (London, 2000).
16 Cercle de Généologie de Mions, 'Histoire de la Soie', http://genealogiemions.free.fr, accessed 28 March 2018.
17 Cited in *Annales de l'agriculture française*, XVII/103–8 (Paris, 1836), p. 163.
18 Faujas de Saint-Fond, cited in *Annales de l'agriculture française*, XVII/103–8 (1836), p. 163. Translation author's own.
19 *Archives Historiques et Statistiques du Département du Rhône* (Lyons, 1825), vol. I, p. 303. Translation author's own.
20 Saint-Fond, cited in *Annales de l'agriculture française*, p. 163. Translation author's own.
21 Serres, *Le théâtre de l'agriculture*, p. 460. Translation author's own.
22 Ibid.
23 John Bonoeil, *His Maiesties Gracious Letter to the Earle of South-Hampton* (London, 1622), p. 2.
24 Alain Pontoppidan, *Le mûrier Actes Sud* (Paris, 2002).
25 Juliette Glikman, *La Belle Histoire des Tuileries* (Paris, 2016).

References

26 Serres, *Le théâtre de l'Agriculture*, p. 457. Translation author's own.
27 M. Loiseleur-Deslongchamps, 'Jardins de France', *Annales de la Société d'horticulture de Paris*, V (1829), p. 293.
28 King James I, *A Counterblaste to Tobacco* (London, 1604).
29 Bonoeil, *His Majesties Gracious Letter*, p. ii.
30 Ibid., p. 2.
31 Herbert Manchester, *The Story of Silk and Cheyney Silks* (Mansfield, CT, 1916).
32 John Feltwell, *The Story of Silk* (Gloucester, 1990).
33 Ibid.
34 William Bartram, *The Travels of William Bartram*, ed. Francis Harper (Athens, GA, and London, 1998).
35 William Farrell, 'Silk and Globalisation in Eighteenth-century London: Commodities, People and Connections c. 1720–1800', PhD thesis, Birkbeck, University of London (London, 2014).
36 Cited in *Archives Historiques*, p. 309. Translation author's own.
37 Ibid.
38 Matthieu Thomé, cited ibid., p. 318. Translation author's own.
39 Matthieu Thomé, *Mémoires sur la Culture du Mûrier Blanc et la Maniere d'élever les Vers à Soie* (Lyons, 1771).
40 Cited in *Archives Historiques*, p. 406. Translation author's own.
41 Georges Guerrard-Samuel Perrottet, 'Morus multicaulis', *Mémoires de la Société Linnéene de Paris* (1825), vol. III, p. 129.
42 Fortune, *A Residence*, pp. 343–4.
43 Comte de Brosse, cited in *Archives Historiques*, p. 19. Translation author's own.
44 John Kitto, *Palestine: The Physical Geography and Natural History of the Holy Land* (London, 1841), p. 237.
45 Edward Joy Morris, *Notes of a Tour through Turkey, Greece, Egypt, Arabia Petraea to the Holy Land*, vol. I (Philadelphia, PA, 1842).
46 Arnold Krochmal, 'The Vanishing White Mulberry of Northern Greece', *Economic Botany*, VIII (April–June 1954), pp. 145–51.
47 Patrick Skahill, *The Cheyney Brothers' Rise in the Silk Industry*, https://connecticuthistory.org, accessed 1 October 2018.
48 R. Govindan, T. K. Narayanaswamy and M. C. Devaiah, *Pebrine Disease of Silkworm* (Bangalore, 1997).
49 Karolina Hutkova, *Silk Connection Between Bengal and Britain: A Story of Complementarity and Political Economy*, Silk and Mulberries Workshop, British Museum, London (23 July 2018).
50 Tessa Morris-Suzuki, *Technology and Culture*, XXXIII (January 1992), pp. 101–12.
51 Claudio Zanier, 'La sericoltura dell'europa mediterranea dalla supremazia mondiale al tracollo: un capitolo della competizione economica tra asia orientale ed Europa', *Quaderni storici Nuova Serie*, XXV/73 (1990).
52 Michio Watanabe, 'Vast, bioclean Kumamoto silkworm factory aims to revive Japan's sericulture sector', *Japan Times* (13 April 2018).

53 Yingnan Xu, 'Chinese Hand-reeled Silk'.
54 Françoise Clavairolle, *Le Magnan et l'Arbre d'Or* (Paris, 2003).

5 Art, Legend and Literature

1 Anne Birrell, *Chinese Mythology: An Introduction* (Baltimore, MD, and London, 1993).
2 Alan L. Miller, 'The Woman Who Married a Horse: Five Ways of Looking at a Chinese Folktale', *Asian Folklore Studies*, LIV (1995), pp. 275–305.
3 Sarah Allan, *The Shape of the Turtle: Myth, Art, and the Cosmos in Early China* (New York, 1991), pp. 41–6.
4 Robert G. Herricks, 'On the Whereabouts and Identity of the Place called "K'ung-Sang" (Hollow Mulberry) in Early Chinese Mythology', *Bulletin of the School of African and Oriental Studies*, LVIII (January 1995), pp. 69–90.
5 Birrell, *Chinese Mythology*, pp. 128–9.
6 Allan, *The Shape of the Turtle*, pp. 27–38.
7 Ibid.
8 Jane Bingham, *Chinese Myths* (London, 2008).
9 Allan, *The Shape of the Turtle*, pp. 41–3.
10 Ibid.
11 Richard Wilhelm, *I Ching; or, Book of Changes*, trans. Cary F. Baynes (London, 1951), p. 53.
12 Plutarch, *The Parallel Lives: The Life of Sulla*, trans. Bernadotte Perrin (New Haven, CT, 1916), p. 2.
13 Joseph Stevenson, trans., *The Church Historians of England* (London, 1853), vol. V, pp. 329–36.
14 Patricia Parker, 'What's in a Name: and More', *Sederi Yearbook*, XI (2002), p. 104.
15 Erasmus, *Praise of Folly* [1511], trans. Betty Radice (London, 1971), p. 56.
16 Peter Bassano, 'Emilia Bassano – Shakespeare's Mistress?', www.peterbassano.com, accessed 1 October 2018.
17 Henry Samuel, 'Van Gogh's ear "was cut off by friend Gauguin with a sword"', *The Telegraph* (4 May 2009).
18 See www.inkyleaves.com.
19 Trisha Parker, personal communication with the author, 12 September 2018.
20 Émile Zola, *The Fortune of the Rougons*, trans. Brian Nelson (London, 2012), p. 5.
21 Claudio Zanier, personal communication with the author, 23 May 2018.
22 Émile Zola, *Dr Pascal*, trans. Vladimir Kean (London, 1957), p. 173.
23 Iman Humaydan Younes, *Wild Mulberries*, trans. Michelle Hartman (London, 2010), p. 44.
24 Alessandro Baricco, *Silk*, trans. Guido Waldman (London, 1997).
25 Elise Valmorbida, *The Madonna of the Mountains* (London, 2018).

26 Elise Valmorbida, personal communication with the author, 25 September 2018.
27 Jeffrey Eugenides, *Middlesex* (London, 2002).
28 Kouta Minamizawa, *Moriculture: Science of Mulberry Cultivation* (Rotterdam, 1997).
29 Monty Don, 'History In Your Garden: Mulberry Tree', *Mail Online*, www.dailymail.co.uk (16 October 2009).
30 James Orchard Halliwell, *Popular Rhymes and Nursery Tales* (London, 1849), p. 126.
31 Ibid., p. 127.

6 Tree of Plenty

1 Daniela Seelenfreund et al., 'Paper Mulberry (*Broussonetia papyrifera*) as a Commensal Model for Human Mobility in Oceania: Anthropological, Botanical and Genetic Considerations', *New Zealand Journal of Botany*, XLVIII (2010), pp. 231–47.
2 Daniel F. Austin, *Florida Ethnobotany* (Boca Raton, FL, 2004), p. 446.
3 Tsien Tsuen-Hsuin, 'Paper and Printing', in *Science and Civilisation in China*, vol. V: *Chemistry and Chemical Technology: Part 1*, ed. Joseph Needham (London, 1985), p. 58.
4 Ibid., p. 1.
5 James A. Millward, *The Silk Road: A Very Short Introduction* (Oxford, 2013).
6 Matthew Jackson, 'The World's Oldest Woodblock Print', https://londonkoreanlinks.net, accessed 4 January 2009.
7 Komila Nabiyeva, 'Uzbekistan Rediscovers Lost Culture in the Craft of Silk Road Paper Makers', *The Guardian*, 2 June 2014.
8 Marco Polo, *The Travels* [c. 1300], trans. Nigel Cliff (London, 2015), p. 124.
9 Ibid.
10 Tsuen-Hsuin, 'Paper and Printing', p. 50.
11 Caroline R. Cartwright, Christina M. Duffy and Helen Wang, 'Microscopical Examination of Fibres used in Ming Dynasty Paper Money', *Technical Research Bulletin*, VIII (2014), pp. 105–16.
12 Ibid., p. 116.
13 Thomas Hardy, *Jude the Obscure* [1896] (London, 1985), p. 184.
14 Plants for a Future, 'Morus alba – L', www.pfaf.org, accessed 1 October 2018.
15 Austin, *Florida Ethnobotany*, p. 446.
16 Victor Hehn, *Cultivated Plants and Domesticated Animals in the Migration from Asia to Europe* (London, 1891), p. 290.
17 Horace, *Satire IV: Odes, Satyrs and Epistles*, trans. Thomas Creech (London, 1720), book II, p. 149.
18 Alexandra Livarda, 'New Temptations? Olive, Cherry and Mulberry in Roman and Medieval Europe', in *Food and Drink in Archaeology*, ed. S. Baker, M. Allen, S. Middle and K. Poole (Totnes, 2008), pp. 73–83.

19 Glaire D. Anderson, *The Islamic Villa in Early Medieval Iberia: Architecture and Court Culture in Umayyad Córdoba* (London, 2013).
20 Walter Scott, *Ivanhoe: A Romance*, ed. Laurence Templeton (London, 1820), chap. 3, n. 4.
21 John Evelyn, *Sylva; or, A Discourse of Forest-trees and the Propagation of Timber*, 4th edn (London, 1706), vol. II, book II, pp. 203–13.
22 Maud Grieve, *A Modern Herbal* (London, 1931), vol. II, p. 561.
23 Evelyn, *Sylva*, p. 48.
24 Olivier de Serres, *The Perfect Use of Silk-wormes, and their Benefit*, trans. Nicholas Geffe (London, 1607), pp. 20–21.
25 Austin, *Florida Ethnobotany*, pp. 446–8.
26 Francis Bacon, *The Works of Francis Bacon* (London, 1740), vol. III, p. 159.
27 M. D. Sánchez, 'Mulberry: An Exceptional Forage Available Almost Worldwide!', www.fao.org, accessed 1 October 2018.
28 'Pekmez – Mulberry, Carob and Grape Syrup', http://turkishcookingeveryday.blogspot.com (July 2011).
29 Plants for a Future, 'Morus alba multicaulis', www.pfaf.org, accessed 1 October 2018.
30 Evelyn, *Sylva*, p. 48.
31 Pliny the Elder, *Natural History*, trans. John Bostock and H. T. Riley (London, 1856), vol. V, book XXX, p. 430.
32 Pliny the Elder, *Natural History*, trans. W.H.S. Jones (London, 1961), vol. VI, book XXIII, p. 507.
33 William Turner, *A New Herball*, ed. George T. L. Chapman et al. (Cambridge, 1995), part II, p. 457.
34 Pliny, *Natural History*, vol. VI, book XXIII, p. 507.
35 George Sfikas, *Medicinal Plants in Greece* (Athens, 1979).
36 Turner, *New Herball*, p. 457.
37 Pliny, *Natural History*, vol. VI, book XXIII, p. 509.
38 Turner, *New Herball*, p. 457
39 Pliny, *Natural History*, vol. VI, book XXIII, p. 507.
40 Joseph Delcourt, ed., *Medicina de quadrupedibus* (Heidelberg, 1914), pp. 6–7.
41 'Mulberry', USDA Food Composition Database, https://ndb.nal.usda, accessed 21 February 2019.
42 Umesh Rudrappa, 'Mulberries Nutrition Facts', www.nutritionandyou.com, accessed 21 February 2019.
43 John Gerard, *The Herball; or, Generall Historie of Plants* (London, 1597), vol II, p. 1508.
44 Attila Hunyadi et al., 'Metabolic Effects of Mulberry Leaves: Exploring Potential Benefits in Type 2 Diabetes and Hyperuricemia', *Evidence Based Complementary Alternative Medicine* (5 December 2013).
45 Simin Tian, Mingmin Tang and Baosheng Zhao, 'Current Anti-diabetes Mechanisms and Clinical Trials Using *Morus alba* L.', *Journal of Traditional Chinese Medical Sciences*, III (January 2016), pp. 3–8.
46 Thomas Moffet, *The Silkwormes and their Flies* (London, 1599), p. 52.
47 Turner, *New Herball*, p. 139.

48 Ibid.
49 Pliny, *Natural History*, vol. VI, book XXIII, p. 507.
50 Aida Se Golpayegani, 'Caractérisation du bois du Mûrier blanc (*Morus alba* L.) en référence à son utilisation dans les luths Iraniens', PhD thesis, University of Montpellier, France (November 2011).
51 Theodore Levin et al., *The Music of Central Asia* (Bloomington, IN, 2016).
52 Laurence Picken, *Folk Music Instruments of Turkey* (London and New York, 1975).
53 Evelyn, *Sylva*, p. 110.
54 Stephen J. Bowe, *Mulberry: The Material Culture of Mulberry Trees* (Liverpool, 2015), p. 11.
55 Cited by J. Lynch, *Becoming Shakespeare* (London, 2007), p. 250.
56 Cowper, *The Task and Other Poems*, ed. Henry Morley (London, Paris, New York and Melbourne, 1899).
57 James Boswell, *The Life of Samuel Johnson, LL.D.* (Oxford, 1886), vol. II, p. 412.
58 Stephen Bowe, 'What Ever Happened to Shakespeare's Mulberry Tree?' www.moruslondinium.org, accessed 23 April 2018.
59 Ibid.
60 Stephen J. Bowe, 'The Most Expensive Wood in the World', *Woodland Heritage* (2015), pp. 14–15.
61 Stephen J. Bowe, 'Why Japanese Mulberry Wood and its Craftsmen are National Treasures', www.moruslondinium.org, accessed 22 February 2017.
62 William Jackson Bean, *Trees and Shrubs Hardy in the British Isles* [1914] (London, 1936), vol. II, p. 84.
63 John Claudius Loudon, *Arboretum et fruticetum britannicum* (London, 1838), p. 1222.

Further Reading

Bowe, Stephen J., *Mulberry: The Material Culture of Mulberry Trees* (Liverpool, 2015)
Campbell-Culver, Maggie, *A Passion for Trees* (London, 2006)
Carey, Frances, *The Tree, Meaning and Myth* (London, 2012)
Feltwell, John, *The Story of Silk* (Gloucester, 1990)
Grieve, Maud, *A Modern Herbal* [1931], vol. II (New York, 1971)
Hehn, Victor, *Cultivated Plants and Domestic Animals in their Migration from Asia to Europe* (London, 1885)
Hemery, Gabriel, and Sarah Simblet, *The New Sylva* (London, 2014)
Huo, Yongkang, *Mulberry Cultivation and Utilization in China* (Rome, 2002)
Kuhn, Dieter, 'Textile Technology: Spinning and Reeling', in *Science and Civilisation in China*, vol. V: *Chemistry and Chemical Technology, Part IX*, ed. Joseph Needham (Cambridge, 1988)
Peck, Linda Levy, *Consuming Splendor: Society and Culture in Seventeenth-century England* (Cambridge, 2005)
Thirsk, Joan, *Alternative Agriculture* (Oxford, 1997)
Whitfield, Susan, *Silk, Slaves, and Stupas* (Oakland, CA, 2018)

Associations and Websites

Ancient Tree Forum
www.ancienttreeforum.co.uk

Bean's Trees and Shrubs: Temperate Woody Plants in Cultivation
www.beanstreesandshrubs.org

Brooklyn Botanic Garden, Brooklyn, NY
www.bbg.org

Monumental Trees
www.monumentaltrees.com

Morus Londinium
www.moruslondinium.org

Royal Botanic Gardens, Kew
www.kew.org

The Plant List
www.theplantlist.org

The Tree Register
www.treeregister.org

United States Department of Agriculture, Plants Database
www.plants.usda.gov

Woodland Trust
www.woodlandtrust.org.uk

Acknowledgements

Many people have helped to bring this book into print after a long gestation. Space will not allow me to mention them all by name. I am particularly grateful to Stephen Bowe, Helen Wang and Susan Whitfield for their invaluable comments on parts of an earlier draft and for their expert support. I can't thank them enough. Any surviving errors or omissions are all mine. Claudio Zanier supplied precious details on mulberry history – and even some Italian mulberry leaves. Caroline Cartwright and Christina Duffy also offered valuable comments on an earlier draft. Paolo Pelosi went to extraordinary lengths to photograph a painting of Francesco Buonvicino in Pescia. Special thanks to David Shreeve and James Coleman of the Conservation Foundation with whom I set up the *Morus Londinium* project on London's mulberry heritage in 2016, with support from the Heritage Lottery Fund. It's been rewarding beyond all expectation. Thanks to Trisha Hardwick, Xanthe Mosley and Jess Shepherd for permission to use their beautiful artwork, and to Lisa Lodwick for help with Roman mulberries and her image of a fossilized pip. Goldsmiths, University of London has given me an office and institutional base for several years. Special thanks to colleagues Les Back, Paul Halliday and Caroline Knowles. Thanks also to David Alderman, Nick Chrimes, Jon Dean, Judy Dowling, John Feltwell, the Gentle Author, Mark Lane, Katy Layton-Jones, Karen Liljenberg, Topher Martyn, Jeremy and Rosie Osborne, Katrina Ramsey, Andrew Stuck, Peter Thomas and Sarah Whale, who have all helped in many ways with my research. Thanks to the supportive staff of the incomparable British Library Map Room. My editor, Michael Leaman, has been impressively patient, giving me nudges and feedback when necessary. Thanks also to Alex Ciobanu, Phoebe Colley and the production team at Reaktion for their support. Many others, too numerous to mention, have also contributed in different ways. Without Jane, Maisie, Louis and Raph, this book would never have been written.

Photo Acknowledgements

The author and publishers wish to express their thanks to the following sources of illustrative material and/or permission to reproduce it. Some locations of artworks are also given below, in the interests of brevity:

AjayTvm/Shutterstock.com: p. 180; courtesy Fabien Bièvre-Perrin/Musée Archéologique de Die et du Diois: p. 172; from Francisco Manuel Blanco, *Flora de Filipinas . . . Gran edición . . .* [*Atlas I*] (Manila, c. 1880–83), courtesy Biblioteca Digital del Real Jardín Botánico, Madrid (CSIC): p. 22; courtesy Joel Bradshaw: p. 16; the British Museum, London: p. 71; from Édouard Chavannes, *Mission archéologique dans la Chine septentrionale*, vol. III (Paris, 1909), courtesy the Digital Silk Road Project, National Institute of Informatics, Tokyo: p. 149; from Wang Chen [王禎], *Nung Shu* (農書, Book of Agriculture), c. 1530: p. 68; photos Peter Coles: pp. 11, 14–15, 21, 24, 25, 26, 34, 38, 39, 42, 47, 48, 86, 94, 99, 107, 110, 186, 201, 204–5, 220; from Walter Crane, *The Baby's Opera* (London and New York, 1877): p. 175; © Jianyi Dai/Food and Agriculture Organization of the United Nations: p. 113; Davison Art Center, Wesleyan University/photo M. Johnston: p. 122; from the *Diamond Sutra* (Dunhuang, 868), British Library, London: p. 183; from Henri-Louis Duhamel du Monceau, *Traité des arbres et arbustes . . . Nouvelle* édition, vol. IV (Paris, 1809), courtesy Biblioteca Digital del Real Jardín Botánico, Madrid (CSIC): p. 46; used by permission of the Folger Shakespeare Library under a Creative Commons Attribution-ShareAlike 4.0 International License (wood no. 11): p. 160; from Robert Fortune, *A Residence Among the Chinese* (London, 1857), courtesy University of California Libraries: p. 114; photo Martin Gee: p. 217; courtesy the Georgia Historical Society: p. 131; courtesy Natasha von Geldern: p. 191; Granger Historical Picture Archive/Alamy Stock Photo: p. 150; courtesy Trisha Hardwick: p. 165; Joseph Jackson Howard and Joseph Lemuel Chester, eds, *The Visitation of London, Anno Domini 1633, 1634, and 1635*, vol. I (London, 1880): p. 161; courtesy J. J. Lally & Co., New York: p. 66; courtesy Lisa Lodwick: p. 91; MARKA/Alamy Stock Photo: p. 174; from Maria Sibylla Merian, *De Europische Insecten* (Amsterdam, 1730): p. 9; Metropolitan Museum of Art, New York: p. 60; courtesy Xanthe Mosley: p. 166; Museo Archeologico Nazionale, Naples: p. 90; Museum of New Zealand Te Papa Tongarewa, Wellington: p. 181; photo Paolo

Pelosi: p. 117; The Picture Art Collection/Alamy Stock Photo: pp. 102, 156; The Pocumtuck Valley Memorial Association Library, Deerfield, MA: p. 139; Pornchan Potinak/Shutterstock.com: p. 56; The Print Collector/Alamy Stock Photo: p. 83; private collection: pp. 8, 37, 81, 167, 168, 176, 192, 196, 208, 219; courtesy Sue Richards: p. 134; courtesy Alan Richardson: p. 29; from Julia Ellen Rogers, *Trees*, in 'The Nature Library' series (Garden City, NY, 1926): p. 44; Royal Commission on the Historical Monuments of England: p. 177; courtesy Carlos Santos Barea: pp. 212, 215; courtesy Liang Shaoji/ShanghART Gallery, Shanghai, China: p. 163; from Charles Arthur Sheffield, *Silk: Its Origin, Culture, and Manufacture* (Florence, MA, 1911): p. 142; courtesy Jess Shepherd: p. 164; from Marc Aurel Stein, *Ruins of Desert Cathay*, vol. 1 (London, 1912): p. 72; photo Sugiyama/S. J. Bowe: pp. 214, 216; from Otto Wilhelm Thomé, *Flora von Deutschland*, vol. 11 (Gera, 1904), courtesy New York Botanical Garden, LuEsther T. Mertz Library: p. 30; © Trustees of the British Museum: p. 185; Universal Images Group North America LLC/Alamy Stock Photo: p. 55; courtesy Andrew Wheeler: p. 57; courtesy Claudio Zanier: pp. 118, 121; from Johannes Zorn, *Icones plantarum medicinalium*, vol. 11 (Nuremberg, 1780), courtesy Harvard Botany Libraries: p. 18.

Nikita, the copyright holder of the image on p. 52, and Forest and Kim Starr, the copyright holders of the image on p. 182, have published them online under conditions imposed by a Creative Commons Attribution 2.0 Generic License. Vahe Martirosyan, the copyright holder of the image on p. 162, has published it online under conditions imposed by a Creative Commons Attribution-Share Alike 2.0 Generic License. Fabien Dany/www.fabiendany.com/www.datka.kg, the copyright holder of the image on p. 84, has published it online under conditions imposed by a Creative Commons Attribution-Share Alike 2.5 Generic License. BabelStone, the copyright holder of the image on p. 55; Bernard Gagnon, the copyright holder of the image on p. 87; JJ Harrison, the copyright holder of the image on p. 33; and David R. Tribble, the copyright holder of the image on p. 43, have published them online under conditions imposed by a Creative Commons Attribution-Share Alike 3.0 Generic License. Didier Descouens, the copyright holder of the image on p. 50; Suyash Dwivedi, the copyright holder of the image on p. 40; Kaidor, the copyright holder of the image on p. 70; David V. Raju, the copyright holder of the image on p. 197; Frullatore Tostapane, the copyright holder of the image on p. 6; Sakaori, the copyright holder of the image on p. 144; San liè [三猎], the copyright holder of the image on p. 75; Soramimi, the copyright holder of the image on p. 145; and Wellcome Collection, the copyright holder of the image on p. 76, have published them online under conditions imposed by a Creative Commons Attribution-Share Alike 4.0 Generic License.

Readers are free to share – to copy, distribute and transmit the work – or to remix – to adapt this image alone – under the following conditions: attribution – you must attribute the work in the manner specified by the author or licensor (but not in any way that suggests that they endorse you or your use of the work); share alike – if you alter, transform, or build upon this work, you may distribute the resulting work only under the same or similar license to this one.

Index

Page numbers in *italics* refer to illustrations

Africa 10, 40, 84, 92–3, 95
age, estimating 10, 13, 16, 27–8, 39, 85, 103–4, 110, 120–21, 138, 157, 178, *180*, 189, 213, 216–21
Aksumite 78–9
Anne of Denmark, Queen 101, *102*, 108
archaeology 58, 63–4, *65*, 70–71, *72*, 89–91, *91*, *149*, 183, 219–21
Archer Yi (Hou Yi) *150*, 151–2
Aristotle 75
axis mundi 8, 147–8
Azerbaijan 38, 189, *207*, 208–9

Bacon, Francis 100, 104–5, 193
Bactria 69, 73, 80, 86
Baricco, Alessandro 171
bark, uses for 17, 21, 48, 161, 179–87, *181*–2, 195, 198–9, 206
Bartram, William 45, 131, 206
Bean, William Jackson 20, 35, 47, 49–50, 217
Becket, Thomas 153–5, 158
Bible 74–5, 86–8, 105, 188–9
Birrell, Anne 147
Black Sea 33, 82, 117
Blackberry (bramble) *8*, 28, 31, 88–9, *175*, 190
Blake, William 13
blood 10, 31, 59, 88, 147, 153–6, 188, 200–203

Bombyx mori 8, *52*, 53–4, 58–67, 69, 73–4, 81, 93, 158, *172*, 203
Bonin *see* Ogasawara
Bonoeil (Bonnel), John 103, 108, 125, 129–30
Bowe, Stephen J. 166, 210, 212, 219
bud 20, 23, *24*–5, 59–60, 200
Buddhism 64, 71, 73, 182–3, *183*
Buonvicino, Francesco 116–17, *117*

Caesar, Julius 89
Cai Lun 181
Cambridge (UK) 13, 103, 220, *220*
Canada 43, 45
Carolina (USA) 45, 131, 206
Cartwright, Caroline 186
Caspian Sea 33, 67, 74, 111
Catholicism 77, 96, 99, 123–4, 128, 132–3, 157
Caucasus Mountains 33, 208
Cecil, Robert 100–105, 217
Central Asia 7, 40, 53, 69, 70, 80–84, 92, 115–17, 145, 147, 189, 207, 209
Charlemagne, Capitulary of 90–91
Charles VIII, king of France 98, 120–21
Chelsea, London 13, 35, 109, *110*, 157, *201*, 218
China 8–17, 20–26, 36–40, 48–58, 63–84, 92, 112–17, 134–7, 144–52, 179–85

Han dynasty 69, 73, 112, 114–15, 152, 181
Huang He (Yellow River) 54, 58, 63, 114
Huzhou 57, 114–15, *114*, 136
Ming dynasty 115, *185*, 186
native species 10, 20, 136, 152, 187, 213
Northern Wei dynasty 114
Qin dynasty 115, 229
Shang dynasty 58, 63, *65*, 148, 152
Sung dynasty 114
Tang dynasty 114, *183*, 186
Warring States period *66*, 67
Yangshao people 55, 58
Yangtze River 37, 114
Yuan dynasty 115, 184, 186
Zhejiang 57–8, 136
climate 20, 23, 76, 91, 106, 108, 114, 124, 131
Cloke, Rene, *Postcard 176*
Colbert, Jean-Baptiste 132
Constantinople 40, 69, 78–80, 83, 95, 116
coppicing 67, 112–15, *114*, 144
Córdoba, Calendar of 190
Cowper, William 211
Crane, Walter, 'Here we go round the mulberry bush' *175*
Cruikshank, George, *The Mulberry Tree 219*
cultivar *see* hybrid

Dandan-Uliq 71–3
diabetes, treatment for 59, 195, 203, 206
Diamond sutra 183, *183*
Domingo, Francisco José, *Morus alba latifolia 22*
dye 78–9, 87, 123, 184, 187–9
Dyke, Zoe Lady Hart 82, 172

Edict of Nantes 96, 109, 124, 132–3
see also Huguenots

Egypt 54, 86, 88
Elizabeth I, queen of England 100, *102*, 104, 217
empire
Arabian (Muslim) 10, 82–4, 92–4, 190
Byzantine 10, 78–83, 93, 95, 116, 138, 140
Mongol 115–17
Ottoman 96
Prussian 134
Roman 10, 34, 74–80, 88–91, *90–91*, 93, 98, 117, 153, 159, 174, 190, 199
Sassanid Persian 33, 73, 79, 81, 84, 86
Erasmus 157
Eugenides, Jeffrey 147, 173
Evelyn, John *107*, 109, 190, 196, 199, 209–10

Faujas de Saint Fonds, Barthélemy 120, 122
Fergana Valley 33, 69, 73, 116
fig 19, 32–3, 35, 46, 87–8, *87*, 93, 158
Florida, colony of (USA) 43, 45, 129, 188, 206
Fortune, Robert *114*, 115, 136
France *50*, 89–90, 96–8, 108, 117, 120–30, 132–5, *134*, 137, 140–41, 145–6, 162–4, *162*, 167–70, *167–8*, 172, 188, 196, 210, 221
Avignon 96–7, 125, 135, 167
Cévennes 97–8, 100, 106, 124–5, 132, 145, 196, 210
Comtat Venaissin 96–7, 132
Languedoc 97–8, 103, 106, 125, 132–3
Lyons 97–8, 121–37, 167
Paris 13, 97, 101, 104, 124–9, *126–7*, 137, 157, 162, 218
Provence 12, 89, 125, 133, 167, *167*
Tours 97, 98, 121, 124–5, 132, 172

Frederick II of Prussia 134, 229
fruit
  drupe *18*, 28–9, *33*, 47, 50
  food 31, 45–6, 189–94
  medicinal uses 10–11, 92, 194, 198–9, 202–3
  furniture 179, 209–10, 213, 215–16

Galen 88, 199
Garrick, David 210–12
Gaul 89–90
Geffe, Nicholas 19, 100, 105, 228
Georgia, colony of (USA) 45, 130–31, *131*, 193
Gerard, John 28, 32, 36, 203
Germany 10, *49*, 90
Greece 93, 95, 208
  ancient 10, 12, 33, 74, 77, 87, 199–200
  Thebes 95–6
Greek, ancient 23, 26, 31, 74, 77, 88, 93, 95, 157, 200, 208
Grieve, Maud 190

Hadfield, Miles 28, 36
Halliwell, James Orchard 175, 177
Harappa, Pakistan 58, 64
Hardwick, Trisha, *Mulberries and Cream* 165, *165*
Hardy, Thomas 187
Hawaii (USA) 180, *182*
Hehn, Victor 87–8, 110–11, 189
Henri II, king of France 123, 227
Henri IV, king of France 98, 100–101, 122–5, *122*, 126–7, *128*, 172–3, 218
Henry VIII, king of England 86, *99*, 99, 109, 157
hermaphrodite 29, 47, 173
Himalaya Mountains 7, 10, 72, *180*
Hinduism 64, 179
Holy Land 88–9, 116
Horace (Quintus Horatius Flaccus) 31, 89, 190
Huangdi, Emperor of China 54–6
Huguenot 96, 109, 123–4, 132–3

hybrid 16, 20, 23, 35–6, 41–2, 45, 50, 155

I Ching 153
India 10, 13, 20, 53, 64, 75, 78–80, 84, 112, 136, 140, 145, 179–80, *180*, *197*, 202, 221
Ishimushi, Kyoshi *215*
Israel 78, 88, 96, 193
Italy *6*, 10, 13, 26, 89, 93, 95–8, 106, 111, 116–23, 125, 132, 143, 169, 171, 173
  Lombardy 117, 119, 125
  Pescia 116, *117*
  Piedmont 12, 119, 123, 131, 134
  Pompeii 34–5, 89–90, *90*
  sericulture 6, 105, 116–20, *117*, *121*, 132, 140, 193
  Venice 95, 115, 161
  see also Sicily

James I, king of England 10, 13, 27, 31, 35, 86, 98–109, *102*, 103–9, 129–33, 159–60, 217–19
Japan
  Izu islands 11–12, 213–17, *214*–17
  sericulture 69, 141–6, *142*–5
  species 11–12, *16*, *17*, 20–21, 36–40, 45, 48, 69, 141–5, *142*–5, 152, 171, 183–4, 187, 194, 207, 221
Jonson, Ben 160
Juniper, Barrie 32, 36
Justinian I, Byzantine emperor 79, 83

kalpavriksha, holy tree 10, 179, *180*
Kazakhstan 92
Keats, John 13
Kew, Royal Botanical Gardens 19, 47–8, *47–8*, 85, 217–18
Khan, Kublai 115, 184, 226
Khotan 70–73, *71–2*, 80
Kichizo company, Japan *216*, *217*
Korea 17, 20–21, 69, 182–4, 213
Kos (Cthos) 77–8
Kunlun Mountains 37, 73, 151
Kyrgyzstan 73, 92

La Salle, Sieur de 180
layering 74, 85, *86*, 98, 136
leaves
 harvesting 10, *55*, *60*, *66*, 67, 68, *76*, *81*, 82, *83*, 114, *118*, 120, *121*, 136, 142–4, *143*, 149, 170–73
 as medicine 193, 195, 198–9, 203, 206
Lebanon 78, 88, 137–8, 170–71,
Leggett, William 54
Leizu (Xi Lingshi) 54–7, 147
Letellier, Jean-Baptiste 61, 101, 130, 227
Levant 86, 133
Loudon, John Claudius 47–9, 106, 218
Louis XI, king of France 97–8
Louis XII, king of France 122
Louis XIII, king of France 128,
Louis XIV, king of France 96, 128 132–3
Low Countries (Netherlands) 104, 120, 133

magnanerie (silkworm house) 103, 109, 124, 128, 130, 137, 140, 145, 167, 220
Médicis, Catherine de 123
Médicis, Marie de 108, 128
Mediterranean Sea 7, 10, 26, 31, 33–4, 67, 74, 78, 82, 86, 92–3, 95, 115–16, 147
Merian, Maria Sibylla, 'Mulberry leaf, silkworm, cocoon' *9*
Merian, Matthäus, *Map of Paris* 127–8
Mexico 93
Middle East 31, 95, 98, 115, 117, 147, 171, 189, 221
Millet, François, *Olivier de Serres* 122
Moffet, Thomas 195, 206
monastery 10, 80, *86*, 90, 98–100, *99*, 154, 162, 221
 see also monk
Mongolia 72, 80
monk 10, 71, 73, 79–82, 99, 154, 182–3
 see also monastery

More, Thomas 109, 157–8, *201*
moriculture
 incentives 97, 112, 114, 119, 121, 130
 integrated farming 9, 53, 113, *113*
 penalties and taxes 87, 93, 112–13, 119, 130
 plantation 10, 13, 101–3, *110*, *114*, 115, 128–9, 131, 136–40, *145*, 169, 171, 221
 roads and hedgerows 13, 133, *134*, *167*–8, 169
 royal gardens 31, 41, 95, 101, 103–5, 108, 123, 125–30, *126*–7, 137, 217–18
 see also sericulture
Morus Londinium project 220
Mosley, Xanthe, *Veteran Morus nigra* 166, *166*
mouthwash 17, 198
multicaulis, species 20, 40–41, 129, 135–40, *139*
murrey, colour 26, 187

Naples, conquest of 120, 122
Nasi, Joseph 96, 227
Native American 45, 129, 180, 188, 191, 199–200, 206
Needham, Joseph 181
Niya (China) 72, *72*
Noguchi, Isamu 183
Normans 93, 95, 218
North America 7, 8, 13, 40, 43–5, *44*, 125, 129, 131, 138, 180, 188, 191, 199–200, 206

Ogasawara Islands (Japan) 16, *16*, 38–9, 45
Ovid 155, 158–9, 167

Pacific Islands 11, 17, 21
Pagani, Gregorio, *Pyramus and Thisbe* 156
Pakistan 51, 58, 64
Palestine 79, 88, 137
Pamir Mountains 73–4, 209
papacy, in France 96

paper 17, 21, 161, 179–84
  hanji 183–4
  money 184–7, *185*
Parker, Patricia 155, 157–8
Pasteur, Louis 140
Pausanias 77, 224
Pennsylvania (USA) 12, 130, 187
Perrottet, Georges Guerrard-Samuel 136
Perry, Matthew C. 38, 39, 141
Persia 7, 10, 12, 26, 31, 72, *75*, 80, 106, 111, 115, 133, 171, 199, 208
Philip IV, king of Spain 96
Philippines, the 93, 136
pleasure garden 31, 101, 108–9
Pliny the Elder 23, *25*, 35, 42, 75, 77, 108, 196–200, 206
Plutarch 153
pollard 13, 32, *134*, 138, 143, 217
pollen, high-speed release 42–3
Polo, Marco 115–16, 184
polyploidy 7, 35–6
Predis, Cristoforo de, *Spherae coelestis et planetarum description 174*
Procopius 79–80
propagation 27, 50, 72, 74, 85, *86*, 124, 136, 209
pun, on *Morus* 155–7
Pyramus and Thisbe 155–9, *156*, 167

Red Sea 78
Redouté, Pierre-Joseph, *Morus rubra* 46
Richthofen, Ferdinand von 70
rights and patents 103, 97, 123, 128–9
ring dance 175, 177–8
Rode, Bernhard, *The Empress of China Culling the First Mulberry Leaves for Silk* 55
Roger II, king of Sicily 95
Rogers, Julia Ellen, *The Red Mulberry* 44
Roland de la Platrière, Jean-Marie 135
root 27–9, 40, 50, 88, 151–3, 171, 174
  as medicine 195–9, 206
Rudrappa, Umesh 202

Saint-Auban, Guy-Pape de 120, 122
Samarkand 73, 116
Schouw, Joakim Frederik 89
seed
  mineralized 34, 90–91, *91*
  smuggled 71, 71–2, 79–81, 91, *91*, 101, 112, 124, 130, 136
Seres 74, 77, 224
sericin (gum) 55, 62, 64
sericulture
  collapse of 13, 140
  gender roles in 60, *66*, 67, 76–7, *76*, 141, 170
  state control of 83, 93
Serres, Olivier de 19–20, 26, 41, 98, 100–101, 105–6, 122, 123–5, 128, 191
Shakespeare, William 31, 158–61, *160*, 210–13
  Emilia Bassano as Dark Lady 160–61
Shaoji, Liang, *Beds/Nature Series No. 10 163*, 164
Sharp, Thomas *160*, 212
Shelley, Percy Bysshe 85
Shepherd, Jess
  040420161613 Mulberry (Morus nigra), 37°11′10.8″N / 3°41′21.2″W 164, 165
Sicily 10, 84, 93, 95, 116, 133, 174, 218
silk
  Cheyney brothers (USA) 139–40
  currency 68, 73
  laws 67, 74
  Lullingstone silk farm (UK) *81*, 173
  mills 132, 140–41, 143
  monopolies 8, 58, 68, 79, 95, 123, 128, 135
  raw 8, 54, 57, 81, 93, 98, 109, *109*, 120–23, 128, 131–3, 139–43
  Raw Silk Company (UK) 109, *110*
  tax on 67, 93, 97, 112–13, 132, 212
  tussah 64, 75–6
silk moth 8, 53–4, 56, 58–9, 62, 64, 66–7, *71*, 75, 141, 160–61, *161*, 173, 203

Silk Road 9, 67–84, *70*, 116, 182, 184, 207
silkworm
  feeding 47, 54, *60*, 105–6, 142
  hatching 59, 61–2, 80, 108, 119
  pébrine disease 138–41, 171, 194
Sixie, Jia 181
Sogdia 73, 82, 86
South America 40, 93, 129
Spain 10, 35, 84, 92–8, *94*, 106, 116, 122, 133, 169, 221
Srellett, E., 'Here we go round the mulberry bush' *8*
Stallenge, William 61, 100–106, 130
Stein, Sir Marc Aurel 70–71, 72, *183*
Straet, Jan van der, *The Gathering of Mulberry Leaves and the Feeding of the Silkworms 60*
sycamore fig *87*, 88, 223
Syria 78, 82, 86, 95–7, 188, 190

Taiwan 49, *51*, 180
Tajikistan 33, 73, 82, 86, *191*
Taklamakan Desert 37, 70, 72–3, *72*
tapa cloth 180, *181*–2
Tarim Basin *see* Khotan
Thanner, B., *Morus nigra L.* *18*
Theophrastus 87
Thirsk, Joan 103
Thomas, Edward 85
Tianshan Mountains 33
Tiberius 74
tobacco 129–30, 139
Tonti, Henri de 180
Tour-du-Pin-de-la-Chaux, Monsieur 120
Tradescant, John (elder) 104–5, 108, 217
Traucat, François 124–5, 227
Tuileries gardens 101, 108, 125, *126*–7, 128, 218
Turkey 11, 26, 140–41, 173, 189, 194, 203, 208 *9*
Turner, William 28, 198–9, 206

Uzbekistan 69, 73, 82, 86, 116, 184

Valmorbida, Elise 173
Van Gogh, Vincent, *The Mulberry Tree* 162, *162*
Verton, François de 103–4
Victoria, queen of England 177–8, 217–18, 220
Virgil 77, 88, 153
Virginia, colony of (USA) 20, 103, 125, 129–30, 132

Walker, Clement 109
weaver, migrant 17, 69, 92–6, 98, 109, 123, 132–3, 139–41, 158, 165, 167
Whitfield, Susan 67, 70, 81
Whitmarsh, Samuel 137, 139
wood
  chatoyance 12, 213, *215*
  furniture and objects 11–12, 179, 206–17, 212, *215*–17
  grain pattern 11, *208*, 210, 213
  musical instrument 207–9, *207*
  shimakuwa 213, *214*–17
Woolf, Virginia 147, 171–2

Yijian, Su 185
Younes, Iman Humaydan 170
Yuezhi people 69

Zanier, Claudio 142
Zhang Qian 69
Zola, Émile 167–70